IMMERSION
Bible Studies

HEBREWS

The Christian life [is]
a journey of transformation
toward communion.

Mary Rose D'Angelo

Acknowledgments

If you can read this book, thank the Rosetown Writers' Group (Margo Day, Debbie McCulloch, Donna Miller, Helen Mourre, Brenda Peters, and Shirley Salkeld). They reviewed parts of it in draft form and made invaluable suggestions. I am the reason there is a saying that there is no good writing, only good rewriting. These gals earned every cent I didn't pay them.

A focus group of kind volunteers from church (Ruth Greer, Kay Olson, Shirley Salkeld, and Elaine Young) helped me to see Hebrews through the eyes of a non-specialist and tease out what actually needed to be said. They also had the good grace to look interested in much of what didn't.

Hazzan (Cantor) Neil Schwartz, spiritual leader of Congregation Agudas Israel in Saskatoon, read through the whole Book of Hebrews in two different translations and offered his observations, as well as responding to specific questions about Judaism. *Todah rabah,* my friend.

Coworkers at my day job (Pat Brisbin, Janae Dawson, Betty-Lou Ernst, Sharon Farrell, Eleanor Head, Gloria Longworth, Diane Machart, and Linda Schaan) helped me keep my feet on the ground and my head in the 21st century.

Roger Kett, my spiritual director through sea changes, laughed uproariously and believed in the unseen.

Editor Stan Purdum offered me the job and stood by me as interpreter and support while I floundered through the unfamiliar waters of contract negotiation.

And Tom, my dearly beloved, found pertinent articles, listened patiently to my ramblings and wrestlings, did his share of the housework, and invariably replied pleasantly to "Oh! What time is it?"

Thank you all.

Praise for IMMERSION

"IMMERSION BIBLE STUDIES is a powerful tool in helping readers to hear God speak through Scripture and to experience a deeper faith as a result."
Adam Hamilton, author of *24 Hours That Changed the World*

"This unique Bible study makes Scripture come alive for students. Through the study, students are invited to move beyond the head into the heart of faith."
Bishop Joseph W. Walker, author of *Love and Intimacy*

"If you're looking for a deeper knowledge and understanding of God's Word, you must dive into IMMERSION BIBLE STUDIES! Whether in a group setting or as an individual, you will experience God and his unconditional love for each of us in a whole new way."
Pete Wilson, founding and senior pastor of Cross Point Church

"This beautiful series helps readers become fluent in the words and thoughts of God, for purposes of illumination, strength building, and developing a closer walk with the One who loves us so."
Laurie Beth Jones, author of *Jesus, CEO* and *The Path*

"I highly commend to you IMMERSION BIBLE STUDIES, which tells us what the Bible teaches and how to apply it personally."
John Ed Mathison, author of *Treasures of the Transformed Life*

"The IMMERSION BIBLE STUDIES series is no less than a game changer. It ignites the purpose and power of Scripture by showing us how to do more than just know God or love God; it gives us the tools to love like God as well."
Shane Stanford, author of *You Can't Do Everything . . . So Do Something*

IMMERSION
Bible Studies
HEBREWS

Chris Ewing-Weisz

Abingdon Press

Nashville

HEBREWS
IMMERSION BIBLE STUDIES
by Chris Ewing-Weisz

Copyright © 2011 by Abingdon Press

Library of Congress Cataloging-in-Publication Data

Ewing-Weisz, Chris, 1958-
  Hebrews / Chris Ewing-Weisz.
      p. cm. -- (Immersion Bible studies)
  ISBN 978-1-4267-0989-0 (alk. paper)
1. Bible. N.T. Hebrews--Textbooks. I. Title.
  BS2775.55.E95 2011
  227'.8707--dc23
                                        2011021120

Editor: Stan Purdum
Leader Guide Writer: John P. "Jack" Gilbert

11 12 13 14 15 16 17 18 19 20—10 9 8 7 6 5 4 3 2 1

Manufactured in the United States of America

Contents

Review Team

Diane Blum
Pastor
East End United Methodist Church
Nashville, Tennessee

Susan Cox
Pastor
McMurry United Methodist Church
Claycomo, Missouri

Margaret Ann Crain
Professor of Christian Education
Garrett-Evangelical Theological Seminary
Evanston, Illinois

Nan Duerling
Curriculum Writer and Editor
Cambridge, Maryland

Paul Escamilla
Pastor and Writer
St. John's United Methodist Church
Austin, Texas

James Hawkins
Pastor and Writer
Smyrna, Delaware

Andrew Johnson
Professor of New Testament
Nazarene Theological Seminary
Kansas City, Missouri

Snehlata Patel
Pastor
Woodrow United Methodist Church
Staten Island, New York

Emerson B. Powery
Professor of New Testament
Messiah College
Grantham, Pennsylvania

Clayton Smith
Pastoral Staff
Church of the Resurrection
Leawood, Kansas

Harold Washington
Professor of Hebrew Bible
Saint Paul School of Theology
Kansas City, Missouri

Carol Wehrheim
Curriculum Writer and Editor
Princeton, New Jersey

Immersion Bible Studies

A fresh new look at the Bible, from beginning to end,
and what it means in your life.

Welcome to IMMERSION!

We've asked some of the leading Bible scholars, teachers, and pastors to help us with a new kind of Bible study. IMMERSION remains true to Scripture but always asks, "Where are you in your life? What do you struggle with? What makes you rejoice?" Then it helps you read the Scriptures to discover their deep, abiding truths. IMMERSION is about God and God's Word, and it is also about you—not just your thoughts, but your feelings and your faith.

In each study you will prayerfully read the Scripture and reflect on it. Then you will engage it in three ways:

Claim Your Story
> Through stories and questions, think about your life, with its struggles and joys.

Enter the Bible Story
> Explore Scripture and consider what God is saying to you.

Live the Story
> Reflect on what you have discovered, and put it into practice in your life.

IMMERSION makes use of an exciting new translation of Scripture, the Common English Bible (CEB). The CEB and IMMERSION BIBLE STUDIES will offer adults:

- the emotional expectation to find the love of God
- the rational expectation to find the knowledge of God
- reliable, genuine, and credible power to transform lives
- clarity of language

Whether you are using the Common English Bible or another translation, IMMERSION BIBLE STUDIES will offer a refreshing plunge into God's Word, your life, and your life with God.

1.

God's Ultimate Messenger

Hebrews 1–2

Claim Your Story

One of my favorite pictures of my dog shows her with her grizzled muzzle lifted toward my face, her sweet brown eyes fixed on mine, paying intent attention. She's not the brightest bulb in the box, but she listens to me.

Dogs listen to their owners. Teenagers listen to their friends. Parents listen to their children. Who do you listen to and how? Do you read your spouse's mind? watch your boss's expression? check your gut to see what you think?

Most of us live with a cacophony of voices demanding our attention—from work and family to telemarketers and movie myths—voices inside us and voices outside us all saying, "Do this!" Sometimes we feel like a dog at a whistlers' convention.

Enter the Bible Story

Introduction

Hebrews invites us to listen to God. More specifically, Hebrews says we should listen to God's ultimate messenger, Jesus.

This may sound obvious, but there are two reasons Hebrews needs to say it. The first is that, well, we don't. Even when we know and believe we should, we take off in our own direction. (Even my sweet and obedient dog who's so eager to please suddenly becomes unable to hear me if there's another dog across the street!)

The other reason the Book of Hebrews needs to talk about listening to Jesus is because at the time the book was written, listening to Jesus wasn't an obvious thing to do at all. Even some Christians were getting wobbly on that point. Most people were not Christians; in fact, they were rather suspicious of Christians, just as we today are suspicious of cults and new religions. Then and now, most people prefer the tried and true: official religions with a long track record adhered to by responsible people in places of power. Some long-haired preacher comes around preaching pipe dreams or revolution, and he's suspect. So the writer of Hebrews not only had to convince his readers, he had to be more convincing than his readers' neighbors, who sometimes used vandalism as a means of persuasion.

We don't actually know a lot about who wrote the Book of Hebrews, to whom, or exactly when. However, we can deduce that it was written late in the first century (probably circa the 60's–90's A.D.) to Jewish Christians who, never having met the earthly Jesus, had learned of him from earlier believers.

These Christians were discouraged and drifting away from the church, perhaps because they were tired of being picked on. Unlike Judaism, Christianity in its first two centuries enjoyed no official status as an approved religion in the Roman Empire. Sometimes there was active government persecution. More commonly, Christians put up with the low-grade hostility of their neighbors and unconverted family members.

This kind of hostility (as any unpopular schoolchild knows) becomes discouraging over time. So it is not surprising that some of these Jewish Christians might have considered giving up on Christianity, especially during flare-ups or threatened flare-ups of persecution, in favor of an officially sanctioned faith that worshiped the same God and featured similar hopes.

Seeing his fellow Christians in danger of jumping ship, one inspired teacher put together a powerful sermon that pulled out all the stops to show why this was not a good idea. That sermon, later passed around as a letter that we now call the Book of Hebrews, has as its central theme the complete superiority of Christianity over Judaism. (We'll talk more about this theme and the problems it raises in Chapter 3, "A New Covenant.")

The Majesty of Jesus

The superiority of Christianity, says Hebrews, begins with the nature of Jesus. He is not just "Son" of God but "firstborn" (1:6). In ancient Near Eastern cultures, the first son in a family automatically received significant privileges and responsibilities that the other children did not. Although all sons (rarely daughters) received an inheritance, the eldest got a double share and became head of the extended family. In a royal house, he succeeded the throne. To prepare for this, his father would invite him to help govern the country, ruling "at the right hand" of the existing monarch.

So to talk about Jesus as God's Son—indeed, his firstborn—is to use a metaphor saying that he is a true and full representative of the Father. A similar meaning is implied when Hebrews applies ideas about Divine Wisdom to Jesus in verses 2 and 3. To Jesus belongs all that God is and has (1:2-4).

Angels, in contrast, are merely messengers and servants of God. The people to whom Hebrews was written believed that angels were powerful spiritual beings and had delivered the Law to Moses at Sinai (2:2), establishing Judaism. Since the writer of Hebrews wanted to encourage Christians not to give up on Jesus and go back to Judaism, he had to show

---

About the Scripture

Psalm 110: The Right Hand of God

When Hebrews 1:3 says that Jesus "sat down at the right side" of God, it is making the first of a number of references to Psalm 110:1, which five other New Testament books also quote. Hebrews will later quote verse 4, too, making it the basis of Hebrews 7. These psalm verses were divine oracles, probably originally addressed to a human king. By Jesus' time, however, they were understood as referring to the coming Messiah. (The Hebrew word *Messiah* and the Greek word *Christ* both mean "anointed." Anointing was how Israel's kings and priests were inducted to office.)

Its messianic meaning made Psalm 110 important to early Christians, who believed that Jesus was that promised one. When Hebrews 1:3 quotes Psalm 110 to say that Jesus "sat down at the right side" of God, the author was saying that Jesus is the Messiah, the divinely ordained King and Priest for all time.

how Jesus and his new covenant are different from (and superior to) the angels and the original covenant. He used a string of Bible quotations (1:5-13), mostly from the Psalms, to contrast what the Scriptures say about the Son with what they say about angels.

The first Christians did not have the New Testament. The books that comprise it were written over a period of approximately 50 years, beginning several decades after Jesus' earthly life. What people did have were the verbal accounts of others who had known, or come to know of, Jesus. They also had the Jewish Bible we now call the Old Testament. (Recall that Jesus and all his early followers were Jewish. With the missionary work of the apostle Paul around 20 years after Jesus' death, significant numbers of non-Jews were welcomed into the Christian church.)

When those first Jewish followers of Jesus read their Bibles, the familiar words came alive with new meaning for them. They saw how the whole sweep of God's dealings with the Israelite people was summed up in the life of Jesus. In him they saw fulfilled the prophets' promises of an ideal king, a Messiah who would bring God's reign on earth.

When those first Christians began to write down the stories of his life, and when missionaries like Paul wrote letters of advice to Christian congregations, their writings were infused with this reimagining of the Jewish Scriptures. Nowhere do we see this more clearly than in the Book of Hebrews. Everything that this book says about Jesus is sourced in the Old Testament; and many analogies are drawn between Israelite history, Law, and worship practices and the new life in Christ. Most importantly, Hebrews talks about the original covenant (or agreement) between God and Israel and how Jesus has mediated a new covenant that brings people much closer to God.

A Reliable Message

If Jesus was no mere angel but the very presence of God among us, then we should listen to him. If the covenant with Israel had been valid and binding (2:2), how much more so the new one. The covenant was received from Jesus the divine Son himself (2:3), with all the reliability and authority that implies. Hebrews then traces a chain of authentication

Hebrews as God's Communication

Hebrews can seem alien and confusing to the modern reader. Although older Bible translations call it the Epistle of Paul to the Hebrews, it's quite unlike Paul's other letters. Nobody knows who wrote it. Whoever it was, clearly he was an educated and cultured person who had meditated long and deeply on the Jewish Scriptures (the early church's Bible). He was also trained in rhetoric and influenced by contemporary intellectual currents, especially by Plato's idea that the world we live in is only a shadowy, imperfect copy of ultimate reality.

Hebrews is so attuned to the dominant Greek culture that it even quotes from the Greek translation of the Old Testament (used by most Jews outside Palestine) instead of the Hebrew original. Yet it often reads like a Jewish *midrash* (commentary).

Clearly, like people today, this writer and his audience were immersed in a stew of interacting and sometimes contradictory influences. Hebrews demonstrates that God speaks through, and to, the assumptions and experiences of every age. The book also shows that we, too, need to interpret our faith in light of our own time as well as in light of the long history of God's work.

from Jesus to the late first-century audience. Since they had not seen Jesus themselves, they relied on the testimony of his original followers, to which God through the Holy Spirit added the experience of signs, wonders, miracles, and spiritual gifts (2:3-4).

Each of us has his or her own chain of authentication. The chain probably begins with people (parents, church leaders, respected friends) who have known Jesus and told us about him. Then we read the Bible and eventually become committed to Jesus ourselves.

Most of us also experience the Holy Spirit's validation. We may not be comfortable with the idea of miracles; but many of us have experienced less dramatic "signs" that, even if we would not trot them out in everyday conversation, have helped us in our spiritual journey. We may have noticed coincidences that underline an important concept or help us make a decision. We may have heard a hymn or been drawn to a Scripture passage that speaks to our need of the moment. We may have felt an inner nudge that helps us find our way through a tangle of conflicting impulses.

In these and so many other ways, God continues to speak, confirming the message of Christ and helping us to live as his disciples.

Yet our access to this confirmation and guidance depends on our ability to trust the messenger. That is why Hebrews lays so much emphasis on the exalted nature of Christ: He was speaking to people who, for whatever reasons, had lost confidence in Jesus and in the Christian message. The writer needed to show that Jesus is God's ultimate messenger.

Truly Human

Jesus' relationship to God is one of powerful identity. His relationship to us is even more astonishing. When the author of Hebrews finally named the pre-existent royal Son who, so far above angels, even created the world, he did not use Paul's usual title of *Christ* (meaning "Messiah"). No, he used the human name *Jesus* (2:9). More than that, just as he spent the entire first chapter insisting on Jesus' identity with God, he gave equal time in the second chapter to insisting on Jesus' identity with us—mere mortal humans.

Indeed, the Book of Hebrews contains the clearest references outside the Gospels to Jesus' earthly life. Unlike the Gospels, however, Hebrews is not interested in Jesus' teaching or in the events of his ministry. The book focuses on just two aspects of his life: his sharing of human nature and his sacrificial death. These are emphasized for a single reason: Both make him uniquely effective as our "great high priest" who gives us access to God and who advocates with God on our behalf.

The discussion of Jesus' death will come much later in the Book of Hebrews. For now it is the nature of his earthly life that is important. The one described in such dazzling terms in Chapter 1 calls us not just "children" (2:13, 14) but "sons and daughters" (2:10) and "brothers and sisters" (2:11, 12), coming from the same Source as Jesus himself (2:11). That's hard enough to take in if you feel loved, never mind if you feel rejected by your family and community as the original readers were. When *you* feel as if you don't belong, how does it help you to know that Jesus calls you a member of his family?

Hebrews says that Jesus can help us because he has lived in our skin. He understands; and in sharing even our death, he broke its power and sprang us from our fears about mortality (2:14-15). Many Christians have in fact died peacefully, trusting that they will soon be with Jesus.

This is why Hebrews says Jesus was made "perfect" through suffering (2:10). It is quite clear that Jesus was never imperfect in the sense of being somehow flawed or incomplete. "Make perfect" (Greek *teleiōsai*, from *telos*, "goal") here means "to fit for a purpose." Jesus' willingness to take on the human condition, to share our mortality and our suffering, is what allows him to accomplish the goal of bringing us with him into the presence of God.

The good news is that's where we ultimately belong. In keeping with what we read throughout the Bible, beginning in Genesis 1:26-27, Hebrews regards human beings highly, as creatures in the image of God, reflecting the divine in a way that the rest of creation does not.

Human sinfulness has given this vision a shadow side. Too often we regard the rest of creation as something to use and abuse. Still, our God-like consciousness does set us apart for responsibility and destiny. Though we may at times feel small and powerless, yet, as Psalm 8 (quoted in Hebrews 2:6-8) says, we are almost angelic in our nature and powers. It has always been God's intention that we be his vice-regents in creation.

Hurricane Katrina, the African AIDS crisis, and the Gulf oil spill remind us that there is still a lot we can't control. "We do not yet see everything in subjection to [humans]" remains as true today as it was 2,000 years ago; "but we do see Jesus" (2:8-9, New Revised Standard Version). He, though undeserving of any suffering, has pioneered the way through loss and death to new life in God's presence. His whole purpose in doing so (2:17-18) was to help us in our losses and dying, tests, temptations, and suffering.

Across the Testaments

Old Testament Roots of Hebrews 1–2

Just about everything Hebrews says is sourced in the Old Testament. Among the writings alluded to are Wisdom of Solomon and, in later chapters, Sirach and 2 Maccabees, found in Catholic Bibles and in some other Bibles as the Apocrypha. Written in between the times of the Old and the New Testaments, these writings are not included in Jewish or Protestant Scriptures but were familiar and influential at the time Hebrews was written.

Because Hebrews uses the Greek translation of the Old Testament (the Septuagint, abbreviated LXX), some quotes in this and subsequent "Old Testament Roots of Hebrews" charts will differ from the text in your Old Testament, which reflects the original Hebrew. *Hebrews 1:2*: Jesus will inherit everything from God.

Hebrews 1:2: God created the world through Jesus.	*Psalm 2:8*: God's anointed will inherit the nations of earth. *Proverbs 8:27-31*: God's Wisdom was present as master worker at Creation.
Hebrews 1:3: Jesus exactly reflects God and powerfully sustains creation.	*Wisdom of Solomon 7:26; 8:1*: Divine Wisdom is a spotless mirror of God and maintains order in creation.
Hebrews 1:3: The Son sat down at God's right hand.	*Psalm 110:1*: God invites the Messiah, a priest/king, to sit at God's right hand.
Hebrews 1:5: [Jesus] named God's Son.	*Psalm 2:7*: Anointed one named God's Son.
Hebrews 1:6: All God's angels must worship [Jesus].	*LXX Deuteronomy 32:43 reads*: "Rejoice, ye heavens, with [God], and let all the angels of God worship him."
Hebrews 1:7: God's angels are winds and flames. [*Angel* means "messenger".]	*Psalm 104:4*: God makes winds and flames his messengers.
Hebrews 1:8-9: [Jesus] the divine Son rules forever in justice and gladness.	*Psalm 45:6-7*: The divinely established king rules forever in justice and gladness.
Hebrews 1:10-12: You, Lord, will outlast your creation.	*Psalm 102:25-27*: God created heaven and earth and will outlast them.

Hebrews 1:13: Jesus sits at God's right hand until his enemies are subdued.	*Psalm 110:1*: God invites the Messiah to sit at his right hand until his enemies are subdued.
Hebrews 1:14: Angels are in God's service for the sake of God's human heirs.	*Psalm 34:7*: God's angel protects those who fear God. *Psalm 91:11*: God commands angels to protect his faithful followers.
Hebrews 2:6-8: The dignity and the destiny of human beings	*Psalm 8:4-6*: The dignity and the destiny of human beings
Hebrews 2:12: Jesus calls us his brothers and sisters and proclaims God to us.	*Psalm 22:22*: [Rescued by God], the psalmist praises God to his faith family.
Hebrews 2:13: Jesus trusts in God.	*Isaiah 8:17; 12:2*: Isaiah waits on and hopes in God and trusts God for salvation.
Hebrews 2:13: Jesus presents himself together with us, the children God gave.	*Isaiah 8:18*: Isaiah and his disciples ("children") are a witness to God in Israel.
Hebrews 2:14: The devil has the power of death.	*Wisdom of Solomon 2:24*: Through the devil's envy, death entered the world.
Hebrews 2:16: Jesus came to help the descendants of Abraham.	*Isaiah 41:8-10*: God will help Israel, the offspring of Abraham.

Live the Story

Like Jesus, the Book of Hebrews is here to help us. Written for disoriented and discouraged Christians who were in danger of losing their way in faith and life, it insists that the remedy for such troubles is a focused effort to deepen faith in Jesus. This may involve grappling with how to understand him in our current culture and circumstances. It certainly will require a choice to turn to him with a trust we may sometimes find hard to feel. We also must learn to listen to him.

Think about how you hear God's voice. Sometimes, something you're reading leaps off the page. A line from a song turns incandescent with meaning. Your thinking shifts during prayer. Maybe you seek God's wisdom in the slow accretion of evidence, or you keep your heart alert for a feeling of inner peace or disturbance. Wise words from a friend or an image that comes to mind can also speak for God.

Hebrews reminds us that the most important ways God speaks to us are through the Scriptures and through Jesus. So bring your attention there. Close your eyes, and take a few deep breaths. Let all the things you've read and thought about Jesus just now swirl around you. Rest with them for a while.

Now turn your attention to God, the God who has spoken and is speaking, has acted and is acting. Is there anything you want to wonder about with God? Is there anything you suspect God may be wanting to say to you? Give thanks for this access you have through Jesus to know God more deeply.

2.

Rest and Resistance

Hebrews 3–6

Claim Your Story

The committee chair looked haggard and was pickier than usual about details. She'd been carrying a lot of responsibility for getting the new housing development off the ground, and it showed. Another key resource person's pallor confirmed the time stamp on the e-mail attendees had received: 2:49 A.M.

Our society is starved for rest. Some of it has to do with the demands and temptations of our 24/7-wired world. Think about what rest means for you: a day away from the cell phone? a full night's sleep? a morning to sleep in? time with your beloved? time alone?

Even with enough sleep, what makes you feel unrested? When are you most frazzled?

Biblical scholar George H. Guthrie maintains that rest is a spiritual issue. Although the demands on us are real, our chronic exhaustion can be as much about self-assertion as anything else. The cure is not so much outside us as inside, where we learn to trust and rely on God.

Enter the Bible Story

Enjoying God's Rest

Hebrews 3–4 meditates on the problem of rest through the lens of a piece of Scripture that would have been familiar to the original audience for Hebrews. That is Psalm 95, which, to this day, is one of the psalms recited at the beginning of the Jewish sabbath service in the synagogue.

As part of the spiritual preparation for worship, the congregation used the psalm to recall God's saving acts and to examine their hearts for any resistance to God. The original readers of Hebrews had probably come to Christianity from Judaism and would have immediately recognized the special function of this psalm when the author quoted it.

Hebrews not only quotes Psalm 95 repeatedly throughout these chapters, but uses it in a question-and-answer history drill (3:16-18). The questions are drawn from the psalm. The answers come from the Bible story it looks back to: the dramatic moment in Numbers 13 and 14 when, on the threshold of the Promised Land, a reconnaissance party brought back a report of a rich but daunting country. The crops were staggeringly abundant, but the towns were strongly fortified and the inhabitants powerful. Most of the spies advised against attempting the conquest; only Caleb and Joshua advocated for pressing ahead.

We can well imagine how confused and frightened the people must have been. After their daring escape from Egypt and their long wilderness journey, perhaps they had expected that God would bring them to a place they could just walk into with minimal resistance. Clearly, however, the takeover would be difficult and dangerous; and the people were not willing to take the risk. They asked instead to go back to Egypt with all the reprisals and reenslavement that was sure to mean (Numbers14:4).

Moses was appalled. His leadership and God's authority had been rejected. He thought God would wipe the people out right there. They had seen the plagues and the parting of the sea. God had provided food and water for them in the wilderness. Yet they did not trust God enough to take bold action to enter the land, so for 40 years they wandered around in the desert until the last of that generation died. Only then could Moses' successor, Joshua, lead them into their inheritance, into the rest they had been promised.

Centuries later, the psalmist meditated on how easily we get in our own way, hardening our hearts against anything that seems too wonderful or too demanding. The author of Hebrews saw his readers sliding into this error. Pulling away from Christianity in a time of difficulty, they were

Old Testament Roots of Hebrews 3–6

Hebrews 3:2, 5: Moses' faithfulness, appointed in God's "house" (Israel)	*Numbers 12:7*: God entrusts Moses with all God's house.
Hebrews 3:7-11, 15; 4:3, 5, 7: Do not harden your hearts as your ancestors did in the wilderness. The disobedient fail to find rest.	*Psalm 95:7b-11*: Do not harden your hearts as your ancestors did in the wilderness. The disobedient fail to find rest.
Hebrews 3:11: God swears the faithless will not enter his rest.	*Numbers 14:20-23*: Though forgiven, the faithless will not enter the land.
Hebrews 3:16-18: The bodies of all who left Egypt, who were rebellious, fell in the wilderness.	*Numbers 14:27-30*: The bodies of those who complained against God will fall in the wilderness, all who left Egypt.
Hebrews 4:4, 10: God rested on the seventh day.	*Genesis 2:2*: God rested on the seventh day.
Hebrews 4:8: If Joshua had given them rest, why mention another day?	*Joshua 22:4*: Following conquest, Joshua tells people God has given rest.
Hebrews 4:12-13: God's word is a piercingly sharp sword revealing truth for God's judgment.	*Wisdom of Solomon 18:15-16*: God's word [at Passover] is a stern warrior with the sharp sword of God's command.
Hebrews 4:12: God's word is a piercingly sharp sword.	*Isaiah 49:2*: God made his servant's mouth like a sharp sword.
Hebrews 5:3: The [Jewish] high priest must offer sacrifices for his sins.	*Leviticus 16:6*: Aaron must offer a bull for his and his family's sins.
Hebrews 5:4: The high priest must be appointed by God.	*Exodus 28:1*: God orders Moses to ordain Aaron and sons as priests.
Hebrews 5:5: Christ is not self-appointed. God named him Son.	*Psalm 2:7*: God names his anointed [Messiah] his Son.

Hebrews 5:6, 10; 6:20: Christ a priest according to the order of Melchizedek.	*Psalm 110:4*: God names his anointed a priest of the order of Melchizedek.
Hebrews 5:7-8: Jesus wept and suffered in obedience to God.	*Isaiah 53:3*: God's servant suffers, experiences human weakness.
Hebrews 6:4-6: Someone who experiences God's goodness and turns away cannot return to grace.	Numbers 14:11-12: The people who rejected God in spite of all the signs done among them should die.
Hebrews 6:13-14: God swore by himself that he would bless Abraham and multiply his descendants.	*Genesis 22:16-17*: God swore by himself that he would bless Abraham and multiply his descendants.
Hebrews 6:15: Abraham obtained the promise by showing patience.	*Genesis 12:1-4; 21:5*: From the first promise to Isaac's birth was 25 years.
Hebrews 6:16: An oath guarantees one's word, shuts down argument.	*Exodus 22:11*: An oath before God shall settle a dispute.
Hebrews 6:18: It's impossible for God to change or to lie.	*Numbers 23:19; 1 Samuel 15:29*: God does not lie or change his mind.
Hebrews 6:19-20: Our hope, like Jesus, has entered the sanctuary behind the curtain.	*Leviticus 16:15-16*: Aaron enters the Holy of Holies behind the curtain to atone for sin.

contemplating going back to their heritage from Moses, thus rejecting the much more trustworthy oversight of Jesus (Hebrews 3:1-6) and risking the loss of a more profound and lasting rest.

Jesus can offer us a much better rest, asserted the author, than the one Moses and Joshua slogged toward. Jesus gives us peace with God, a deeper and more secure peace than that afforded by the law of Moses (3:5-6; 8:6; 10:11-17); and in the end he brings us into the eternal "sabbath rest" of God (4:9-10). We can be sure of this rest. Jesus has pioneered the way into it (4:10, 6:19-20); but it is only ours if we believe in it, if we accept it.

Lack of faith and other kinds of disobedience can prevent us from enjoying God's rest (4:11), but it is always there to be had. Indeed, by a delightful rabbinic kind of logic, God's rest has been available from the beginning of time. In Genesis 1:1–2:3, the account of the seventh day, unlike the others, wasn't closed off by saying, "And there was evening and there was morning, the Nth day." Thus, the rabbis surmised, the seventh day, God's resting day, must still be going on! This is what the author of Hebrews was referring to in 4:3b-4. (We will see a similar kind of logic in the discussion of Melchizedek in Hebrews 7:3.)

Whenever We Are in Need

No wonder, then, that Hebrews urges us to "make every effort to enter that rest so that no one will fall by following the [Israelites'] example of disobedience" (4:11). Who on earth would ever turn down rest? However, it can be hard to know God's will and easy to deceive ourselves about whether we're doing it.

God has provided two wonderful gifts to help us. One is the Word, as alive and penetrating as God's own self (4:12-13), helping us see through our sinfulness and find the path of obedience. Whether it is the Bible that is in view here or Christ the Living Word, we can be sure that our faithful attention to the Scriptures and prayer will allow the Holy Spirit to bring God's word for us into contact with our lives and circumstances.

Because the reality is that we will at times fail in our obedience, God has also provided Jesus, our great high priest (4:14), to offer forgiveness and to walk us through to renewed faithfulness. He was not born into the priestly family of Aaron, but he does fulfill the deeper requirements of priesthood: He was taken from among the people he represented, he shared their humanity, and he was appointed by God rather than self-appointed (5:1-10).

Although the full exposition of Jesus' priesthood is reserved for a later chapter, Hebrews does tell us something important here. Instead of offering sacrificial animals on behalf of the people, what Jesus offered was "prayers and requests with loud cries and tears" (5:7). This seems to refer particularly to his wrenching struggle in Gethsemane to accept God's will (Matthew 26:36-46). His obedience to God and his compassion for us reach a peak here that supremely exceeds what any other priest or sacrifice could do. This supremacy of sacrifice, along with his deep

About the Scripture

Day of Atonement

In Hebrews 5:3, we find the first allusion to what will shortly become central to the book's argument: the rituals of the Jewish Day of Atonement (Yom Kippur). Chapters 8–10 compare the instructions for celebrating the first Day of Atonement in the portable worship tent in the wilderness, with the work of Jesus. The Day of Atonement (Leviticus 16) required the high priest to sacrifice animals and bring their blood into the holiest part of the tent to atone for his sins and those of the people. He also symbolically laid the people's sins on a goat that was then driven into the wilderness (the "scapegoat"). There were rituals to purify the priest and the worship area, too.

Prayers replaced the sacrifices after the Temple was destroyed in A.D. 70, but Jews still observe Yom Kippur annually. Contrary to Hebrews 7:27 and 10:11, there were never daily sacrifices for sins. The daily offerings were for worship.

understanding born of sharing our reality, is what impels our author to encourage us, whatever our need, to come unhesitatingly to Jesus for help (Hebrews 4:16).

A Call to Maturity

Jesus does not, however, simply wave a magic wand and make rest for us happen. We still have to go there of our own choice, and it is a choice that requires effort. The frustration that has bubbled under the surface of these chapters breaks out here: "We have a lot to say about this topic, and it's difficult to explain, because you have been lazy and you haven't been listening" (5:11).

It isn't enough to sit on our salvation. Life in God demands our active participation. Indeed, the church needs teachers, people of mature faith who can show the way to others; and that takes sustained practice. Just as nursing babies have to grow up into children who can eat more and do more, and finally into adults who take responsibility and raise the next generation, so Christians need to move on from the basics of salvation into a more robust and nuanced faith that is equal to the challenges of life.

Unfortunately, the author feared that his readers were not maturing —indeed, they were in danger of falling away from Jesus altogether. No matter how understandable that might be in a time of persecution, Hebrews insists that it isn't just one more human lapse. Don't count on coming back to Jesus as if nothing had happened, he warned. In fact, you shouldn't count on being able to come back at all (6:4-8).

Christians through the centuries have struggled with this passage. It is so harsh! Indeed, the tone of these verses almost cost Hebrews its place in the Bible, because of its similarity to the rigorist position of certain

About the Scripture

The Bible as We Know It

The Bible we have today is composed of many books written by many different people over the course of many centuries. How did certain works come to be recognized as God's word to us, while others are simply useful and interesting? It is the collective judgment of God's people over a long period of time that has established the canon of Scripture.

The Hebrew Bible, or Old Testament, had been firmly recognized in its present form for a century or more by the time Jesus was born. It was to this established Scripture that early Christians turned for guidance when they were working out how to understand him.

For information about Jesus' life and teachings, people relied on the testimony of the apostles (the twelve disciples and Paul), who were still living during the first decades of the church. For the most part, this teaching circulated orally.

The first writings of what later became the New Testament were the letters that Paul wrote to various churches to address specific situations. The Gospels and other writings came later. None of these was initially regarded as Scripture (God's authoritative word). They were considered only as a faithful record of Christian teaching.

During the second century, however, as the split between Christians and Jews became final, the apostles died, and heresies arose, it became necessary to identify which Christian writings accurately portrayed God's work in Christ. By this time, the four Gospels and the letters of Paul were widely recognized as the Word of God. Other writings took longer to gain acceptance or to be rejected definitively as Scripture, but the New Testament as we know it today was recognized by the end of the fourth century. A council that met in Carthage in A.D. 397 formally approved the canon we know, finalizing a long period of discernment.

heretical groups in the third and fourth centuries. However, Hebrews' point is well taken: To have fully experienced the Christian life (6:4-5) and then to turn away from Jesus is not a small matter. It not only devalues him, it could be seen as participation in the malice of those who crucified him in the first place.

If you are struggling with doubt, words like these can seem not only frightening but unfair. Ultimately, it is not Hebrews that judges us. It is our merciful high priest, Jesus, who understands us better than we understand ourselves. However, if we count on his mercy, we must also count on his penetrating truthfulness.

Doubt is not sinful in itself; it is often the road by which we "[move] on from the basics" (6:1) into more mature understanding and obedience. However, doubt allowed to fester, and behavior that distances us from God and from God's people, can take us where neither we nor Jesus would ever want to see us go. The writer of Hebrews hastened to assure his first audience that he was sure they had not reached such a dire point, but he clearly believed it was possible. That is why he reiterated the need for persistence, for making faithfulness a habit (6:12). "We desperately want each of you to show the same effort to make your hope sure until the end" (6:11).

After such unnerving severity, it is doubly sweet to hear the words of assurance with which the chapter closes. Though we ourselves are unreliable, our salvation does not rest on us alone; it rests ultimately on the faithfulness of God, and about that there can be no question. Knowing our need for reassurance, God does not merely promise to be our God—a promise secure in itself, since it rests on the unchanging nature of God—but also confirms that promise with an oath. "He did this so that we, who have taken refuge in him, can be encouraged to grasp the hope that is lying in front of us," a hope that is "a safe and secure anchor for our whole being" (6:18-19).

A Bible Timeline

Knowing the sequence of Bible-related events makes Hebrews easier to follow. Dates are approximate. The date of the Exodus from Egypt is especially uncertain (estimates range from 1550 to 1210 B.C.).

2000 B.C.:	Abraham trusts God for land and descendants. Abraham meets Melchizedek.
1800 B.C.:	Jacob and his descendants become the tribes of Israel.
1290 B.C.(?):	Moses leads Israelites from Egypt to edge of Promised Land. *Mount Sinai*: Ten Commandments, first covenant and Law; *Wilderness wanderings*: worship in the Tent of Meeting
1250 B.C.(?):	Joshua leads Israelites into the Promised Land. Period of conquest and settlement under judges
1000 B.C.:	King David is Israel's greatest king. Many psalms and prophetic books are written over next 600 years.
587 B.C.:	Military defeat and exile end Israel's independence. Some Israelites return and rebuild beginning in 538 B.C.
333 B.C.:	Alexander the Great establishes Greek rule in Palestine. Greek culture becomes the norm around the Mediterranean.
166 B.C.:	Jewish revolt and independence under the Maccabees
63 B.C.:	Pompey establishes Roman rule in Palestine.
6 B.C.–A.D. 27:	Birth, ministry, death, and resurrection of Jesus
A.D. 40–65:	Christian churches welcome many non-Jews as well as Jews. Apostle Paul's missionary work and letters
A.D. 64–68:	Persecution of Christians by Roman emperor Nero
A.D. 60–95:	Period in which Hebrews was probably written
A.D. 66–70:	Jewish revolt, crushed by Rome; Jerusalem Temple destroyed. Gospels and other New Testament books written in next 40 years.

Live the Story

Do you know the hymn "Trust and Obey"? If you rummage around at your church, you can probably find it in an old gospel collection. The chorus tells the truth: "Trust and obey, for there's no other way / to be happy in Jesus, but to trust and obey." To be anchored securely, so that we can have rest, requires trust and obedience.

Read or hum this hymn, and notice what comes up for you. Gratitude? hurt or anger? resistance to the idea of obedience? difficulty trusting? memories? skepticism? present struggles? Take a few moments to reflect on your reaction and to examine your heart. Have you been lazy in your Christian development, or are you pushing ahead in understanding and service? Have you been finding rest, or do you need help? Talk it over with Jesus, who is always ready to listen and to help in time of need.

A trusting and obedient faith is the key that makes us the recipients of God's promises, which are fulfilled in life today and in eternity.

3.

A New Covenant

Hebrews 7:1–10:18

Claim Your Story

How did you first come to know God? Perhaps your mother coached you in childish bedtime prayers to "bless Mommy and Daddy and Susie and Spot." Maybe you went to Sunday school singing "Jesus Loves Me" and watching flannelgraph Bible stories or Veggie Tales videos. Or was God a more distant concept, not part of your life, until a charismatic preacher or a life crisis propelled you into a passionate quest?

No doubt your way of understanding and relating to God has changed over time, just as your relationships with human friends develop and change. Maturing thought and the experiences you have lived through have probably modified the way you look at the world and at God. Perhaps you have come closer to God. Maybe you have pushed away in anger or doubt. Maybe you've done both at different times.

It is not only individuals whose relationship to God develops and changes. The Bible chronicles many ups and downs and shifts in perspective in the collective story of God's people. The most radical of these was when a growing group of Jews became convinced that Jesus was the Messiah and eventually moved away to form a whole new religion, Christianity, with its own Scriptures (the New Testament) and an un-Jewish understanding of the Jewish Scriptures of the Old Testament.

Enter the Bible Story

A New Covenant

Hebrews 7–10 goes back to the very foundation of Judaism and talks about how it looks through the lens of commitment to Jesus. These chapters are confusing for the modern reader since they assume knowledge and beliefs that are no longer current. Literal translations of the Bible, such as the CEB, do not have the freedom of using idioms that can convey the original meaning of the text. Reading good paraphrased editions or amplified Bibles and studying good commentaries will assist in understanding the train of thought in these chapters and would be worth your while to read if you would like to better understand the details.

Judaism is founded on the belief that God established a special relationship, or covenant, with Abraham. God promised the elderly, childless Mesopotamian a new homeland and offspring; and he promised Abraham that through his family all the earth would be blessed (Genesis 12:1-3).

Eventually, from this improbable beginning came the people of Israel, whom Moses led from Egyptian slavery to the land that now bears their name. On the way from Egypt to the Promised Land, the fledgling nation camped near Mount Sinai, where they received not just the Ten Commandments but the entire body of Jewish law, including instructions for worship and daily life. This Torah, or Law, specified the shape of their covenant relationship to God.

Jewish rabbis and scholars down through the ages have adapted the regulations to changing conditions, enabling the community to continue to bring God's justice and holiness into everyday life. The covenant thus remains for Jews alive and valid.

The followers of Jesus, however, perceived God doing something altogether new, instituting a whole new covenant. In one sense, it was the same original covenant, unfolding to its full magnificence when the time was ripe. In another way, though, it was new, bringing new means, new scope, and new results to an old partnership.

A Different Kind of Priest

The awesome experience of Mount Sinai had made God seem dangerous and unapproachable. The laws setting out the physical structure of the worship tent and the annual Day of Atonement ritual (briefly summarized in Hebrews 9:1-7) served to emphasize this sense of the separation that sin creates. In Jesus, however, people experienced God coming close to them, welcoming them, and setting aside barriers.

Although Jesus was not a priest, and in fact was not qualified to be one under Jewish law, people experienced him doing what priests were intended to do: help them approach God. This, combined with the fact that the Messiah is described in Psalm 110 as being a priest as well as a king, must have prompted the author of Hebrews to plumb his heritage for ways to talk about the priestly ministry of Jesus.

Psalm 110:4 says that the Messiah will be "a priest forever, according to the order of Melchizedek" (NRSV). This takes us back centuries before Sinai (Genesis 14:18; see the Bible Timeline in Chapter 2), to Abraham's encounter with a priest-king named Melchizedek. Unlike the later priests of Israel, whose priesthood depended on belonging to the tribe of Levi, Melchizedek's ancestry is unknown. Since Genesis doesn't mention his forebears or successors, and since the great Abraham recognized him as a superior, he became mythologized as supernatural and eternal—the ultimate priest of Almighty God.

That is why the psalm speaks of the Messiah being like Melchizedek and why the author of Hebrews applied the description to Jesus. "He has become a priest by the power of a life that can't be destroyed, rather than a legal requirement about physical descent" (Hebrews 7:16).

From Psalm 110, Hebrews also picks up the detail that the Messiah is made priest forever by God's oath. This implies that a new covenant is being enacted, for covenants must be sealed with an oath. Since a change in the priesthood represents a change in the terms of the covenant (Hebrews 7:12), this makes sense. Jesus, the new and eternal priest, also brings in a new covenant, a new way of relating to God. This new covenant is not based on law or regulations but on hope (7:18-19).

About the Scripture

Priests in Antiquity

In Israel, under the terms of the Sinai covenant, only men born into the tribe of Levi could serve as priests or Temple staff. Aaron, the first high priest, was a member of the tribe of Levi; and all subsequent high priests had to come from Aaron's family. Jesus was born into the tribe of Judah, so he was not qualified under Jewish law to be a priest of any kind—let alone high priest. However, as a member of the tribe to which King David had belonged, and in fact a direct descendant of David, he did qualify to be the Messiah, who was expected to be a royal, not a priestly, figure.

In Israel, king and priest were separate offices. This was not always so in other cultures. Hebrews 7 talks about Melchizedek, who was a king (perhaps of the city that later became Jerusalem) and a priest of "the Most High God" (Hebrews 7:1; Genesis 14:18). We don't know what culture or religion he belonged to. Since Judaism did not yet exist, he was not Jewish. However, Abraham recognized him as worthy of respect, and that is how he came to be a figure in Jewish lore.

The author of Hebrews (like Paul in Galatians 3:10-11 and Romans 7:14-18) recognized that no human being can ever completely keep the Law. However, because Jesus did completely embody God's will and offered his obedience as a sacrifice on our behalf (Hebrews 7:26-27), we can approach God through him and not on the strength of our own goodness. This hope is our anchor (6:19).

Shadows and Substance

People have always needed hope. Long before Jesus' time—when the nation of Judah was falling apart, around the start of the sixth century B.C. —people were afraid they had sinned so badly that God had rejected them forever. The prophet Jeremiah spoke words of hope and comfort to them: There would be a new covenant of deepened intimacy. They would still be the people of God. Indeed, they would be bound to God mind to mind and heart to heart, their sins forgotten.

To the first Christians, this promise took on a startling new resonance: Jesus was the key to God's new covenant. He had done what the old Law and sacrifices could not do: cleanse people to the core and bring them into a confident relationship with God. Everything that had come before was like a shadow cast by him, a mere copy of the heavenly original. They saw that Jesus fulfilled and transcended all that the old covenant offered.

Why All That Blood?

Hebrews talks a lot about the need for sacrifices. This is because the Jewish covenant (like other religions of the time) called for many of them. Every morning and every evening, meat, grain, and wine were offered as "a pleasing odor to the LORD" (Numbers 28:1-8, NRSV). There were extra offerings on the sabbath. At the beginning of each month and on the annual festivals, there were more of these worship offerings as well as a single male goat offered for sins.

Once a year, on the Day of Atonement, along with extra worship offerings, there were special sacrifices and rituals to cleanse priest and people from unintentional sins. Sacrifices were also used to ratify and renew covenants. Everyone assumed that sacrifices were an essential part of approaching God.

Unfortunately, Hebrews creates the impression in these chapters that Judaism is all about purity and fruitless attempts to atone for sin. This is not true. The sacrificial system was a nuanced approach to the many aspects of fellowship with God and of life in community. Everything in Christianity flowers from these roots.

Still, even within Judaism, there was a growing recognition that there was a limit to what an animal sacrifice could accomplish. (Modern Jews regard sacrifice as having been a stage along the way to approaching God through prayer.) The psalms and prophets are peppered with acknowledgments that what God seeks is obedience—not just the correct offering brought at the correct time, but a whole life lived in accord with God's vision for a just society. Hebrews quotes one of these passages (Psalm 40:6-8) in 10:5-7 and says that Jesus' ultimate offering was his obedient life. That is what makes his blood superior to that of animals (9:13-14; 10:9).

To modern Western ears, Hebrews' emphasis on blood is puzzling and off-putting. However, blood sacrifice has a long and world-spanning history as a way of approaching and entering into relationship with the divine. Even today, various cultures feature animal sacrifice. This is probably because, as Leviticus 17:11 says, blood is the very life of a creature; it signifies ultimate importance.

About the Scripture

Jews and Christians

Christianity originated as a sect within Judaism whose members believed Jesus was the long-awaited Messiah. Most Jews disagreed. He had failed to do what the Messiah was promised to do: reunite and purify Israel and end foreign domination. By the second half of the first Christian century, both Christians and Jews began to recognize that Christianity was no longer part of Judaism. The dividing household of faith was full of conflict and harsh words.

The early church, like a teenager, defined itself mostly in opposition to its parent. Unfortunately, this turbulent period is when the New Testament was written. Hebrews, like other parts of the New Testament, contrasts Judaism and Christianity—not always fairly or accurately—and insists that Christianity is the only legitimate successor to the Hebrew Bible tradition.

Because Hebrews addresses Jewish Christians who were tempted to abandon Christ, the author was categorical that the old covenant was finished (8:13). The apostle Paul, writing to smooth tensions in a mixed Jewish and Gentile Christian congregation, took a more measured approach in Romans 9–11. He, too, believed that, finally, all must come to Christ; but he could not believe that God's covenant with Israel could ever be annulled. While waiting for God to work out the details, he cautioned non-Jewish Christians against arrogance. God's covenant with Israel is the enduring root onto which others have graciously been grafted (Romans 11:17-18).

In our time, a spirit of curiosity, respect, and willingness to learn not only about the faith of others but about the context and challenges in which it is lived, seems an appropriate exercise in following Jesus, who lived, died, and was resurrected a Jew.

Because of the role of sacrifices in making covenants, Hebrews 9, recalling the rituals at Sinai, speaks of the "blood of the covenant." Emphasizing the life-and-death importance of a covenant with God, the chapter also explores the multiple meanings of the word. The usual New Testament word for covenant is *diathēkē*; but for Greek-speaking people living all over the ancient world, the everyday meaning of this word was the legal document we call a "will." Like Paul in Galatians 3:15-18, the author of Hebrews found this double meaning resonant. A death was required to ratify either a will or a covenant, and both involved stipulations and benefits. Whichever way you understand *diathēkē*, Jesus' self-offering is uniquely powerful in giving us access to its provisions.

With Jesus' death and resurrection, says Hebrews, the need for sacrifices ended. Whether for sin or for any of the other needs that sacrifice addressed, we are invited to approach God confidently through our living high priest on the basis of his once-for-all work. Walking daily with him allows us to grow into the same kind of trusting and responsive relationship that he has with God, making the new covenant real.

Across the Testaments

Old Testament Roots of Hebrews 7:1–10:18

Hebrews 7:1-3: Abraham's encounter with Melchizedek after defeating the kings	*Genesis 14:17-20*: Abraham's encounter with Melchizedek [defeating kings: Genesis 14:1-16]
Hebrews 7:3: A priest for all time	*Psalm 110:4*: Melchizedek is a priest forever.
Hebrews 7:5: Levitical priests receive a tenth.	*Numbers 18:21*: The Levites receive a tithe (tenth).
Hebrews 7:11: Why would God speak of raising up another priest according to the order of Melchizedek?	*Psalm 110:4*: God has sworn: You are a priest forever, according to the order of Melchizedek.
Hebrews 7:16-17: Jesus is priest by the power of a life that can't be destroyed, like Melchizedek.	*Psalm 110:4*: You are a priest forever, according to the order of Melchizedek.
Hebrews 7:21: Jesus' priesthood was affirmed with God's oath.	*Psalm 110:4*: God has sworn and will not change his mind. You are a priest forever.

	Leviticus 16:6, 15: On the [annual] Day of Atonement, the high priest sacrifices for his and the people's sins.
Hebrews 7:27: Jesus doesn't have to offer sacrifices daily for his and the people's sins.	*Leviticus 4:1–6:7*: Instructions for sin offerings made on an as-need basis for individual trespass.
	Numbers 28–29: The daily, monthly, and festival offerings, most for worship, not sin [no daily sin offering].
Hebrews 8:1: Our priest sits at the right hand of God's throne.	*Psalm 110:1*: God invites the priest-king to sit at God's right hand until enemies are subdued.
Hebrews 8:5: Moses was warned by God to follow the heavenly pattern for the meeting tent.	*Exodus 25:40*: See that you make (the tent and its furnishings) according to the pattern shown on [Sinai].
Hebrews 8:8-12: A new covenant with God	*Jeremiah 31:31-34*: A new covenant with God
Hebrews 9:1-5: A description of the holy place on earth (the tent of meeting) and its furnishings	*Exodus 25-26*: The meeting tent and its furnishings
	Exodus 16:33: The jar of manna
	Numbers 17:1-10: Aaron's rod that budded
Hebrews 9:6: Priests enter the tent all the time as they perform their service.	*Leviticus 24:1-9*: Regular priestly duties in the tent include tending the lamp and the bread.
Hebrews 9:7: Only the high priest enters the holy of holies, just once a year, with blood.	*Leviticus 16*: Day of Atonement instructions (See especially verses 2, 14-15, 34.)
Hebrews 9:13: The blood of goats and bulls and the sprinkled ashes of cows	*Leviticus 16:14-15*: A bull (for the priests) and a goat (for the people) were the Day of Atonement sin offerings.
	Numbers 19:1-13: Ashes of a red heifer were used to purify people from contact with dead bodies.

Hebrews 9:14: Jesus a sacrifice without any flaw	*Leviticus 4:3*: The bull for the sin offering [like all sacrifices] must be without blemish.
Hebrews 9:19-20: Moses used calf and goat blood, water, scarlet wool, and hyssop to sprinkle the Law scroll and the people: blood of the covenant.	*Exodus 24:3-8*: Moses sprinkled blood on the altar and on the people: blood of the covenant. *Leviticus 14:6; Numbers 19:6, 17-18*: Water, scarlet wool, and hyssop were used in cleansing rituals [not at Sinai].
Hebrews 9:21: Moses sprinkled the meeting tent and priestly equipment with blood.	*Leviticus 8:15*: At Aaron's ordination, the altar was consecrated and purified with blood. *Numbers 7:1*: The meeting tent, furnishings, altar, and equipment were consecrated by anointing [with oil].
Hebrews 9:22: There is no forgiveness without blood.	*Leviticus 17:11*: Blood is given for making atonement.
Hebrews 9:28: Christ was offered once to take on himself the sins of many people.	*Isaiah 53:12*: God's servant poured himself out to death and bore the sins of many.
Hebrews 10:4: It's impossible for the blood of bulls and goats to take away sins.	*1 Samuel 15:22*: To obey is better than sacrifice. (Similarly, Psalm 40:6-8; 50:8-15; 51:16-19; Isaiah 1:11-17; Jeremiah 6:19-20; 7:22-23; Hosea 6:6; Amos 5:21-24; Micah 6:6-8.)
Hebrews 10:5-7: You didn't want a sacrifice; I have come to do your will.	*Psalm 40:6-8*: You didn't want a sacrifice; I have come to do your will.
Hebrews 10:5: You prepared a body for me.	*LXX Psalm 40:6* reads: "Sacrifice and offering thou wouldest not; but a body hast thou prepared for me."
Hebrews 10:12-13: Jesus sits at God's right hand, waiting for his enemies to be subdued.	*Psalm 110:1*: The LORD says to my master: / "Sit right beside me / until I make your enemies a your footstool for your feet!"
Hebrews 10:16-17: This is the [new] covenant: I will place my laws in their hearts, forget their sins.	*Jeremiah 31:33-34*: This is the [new] covenant: I will place my laws in their hearts, forget their sins.

Live the Story

The overall point of this session is that God's gift of Jesus Christ to the world brings righteousness in place of sinfulness and joy in place of punishment. These chapters of Hebrews help us to envision that.

Hebrews 10:19-22 invites us to follow Jesus right into the heavenly holy place, the presence of God, and to experience the freedom to live confidently for God in the world. Does that seem like a good description of the kind of relationship you have with God at this time? Why or why not? Would you change anything about the present state of your Christian life?

Turn to the description of the new covenant in Hebrews 8:8-12. Read it slowly and prayerfully, pausing on any word or phrase that especially speaks to you. Ask the Holy Spirit to suggest a perspective or action that will help you grow in your relationship with God this week.

4.

Promise and Pain

Hebrews 10:19-39

Claim Your Story

Human beings are born to trouble as surely as sparks fly upward, lamented Job 5:7 several millennia ago. Our circumstances, our relationships, even our successes can deliver wave upon wave of challenge and pain, so that we wonder sometimes whether we can keep going or whether it's all worth it.

Think about a time when you were hurt or discouraged, when your confidence took a beating, when you couldn't find a way forward. Probably you were tempted to turn into a hard little ball so you couldn't be touched, or to blow up in a rage to keep the danger at bay. Maybe you crawled under a haze of alcohol, drugs, television, or food for comfort. What does it mean, in such a time, to have faith? How do you access Jesus' "new and living way" (Hebrews 10:20) into the resources of God's presence? What help can you expect to find?

New Testament scholar Donald Guthrie, writing about this part of Hebrews, notes that it is a mark of the mature Christian to understand God's will in a way that makes room for adverse events. Life is what it is, and God doesn't change that. Instead, as the first few chapters of Hebrews so richly describe, God enters life-as-it-is with us. God in Jesus Christ shares our existence fully, experiencing our suffering, our tears, even our death.

It is through this full humanity of Jesus (abbreviated as "his body" in 10:20) that we can come fully into the presence of God. Instead of being the barrier it used to be (the "curtain" in front of the Holy of Holies, 10:20), our humanity becomes the point of connection with Christ that allows us to draw on God's wholeness and to take his divine nature back into our difficult daily lives.

Enter the Bible Story

The CliffsNotes *Hebrews*

This short half-chapter of Hebrews (10:19-39) is the *CliffsNotes* form of the book as a whole. In it, we find a brief summary of everything the author had been driving at throughout the book, as well as the most intense expression of his pastoral concern for the people in his audience. Remember that these were people who were tempted to give up on Christianity. They were drifting away from active participation in their church (10:25) and wearying of the social hostility (10:32-34; 12:3-4) that came with belonging to a suspect new religion.

It would have been so easy to go back home to Judaism. Whatever it was that had drawn them to Christ in the first place was fading to insignificance in the face of their current difficulties. Perhaps there are times when you have felt the same—when it seemed your faith was doing you no good at all, and maybe even adding to your problems.

Act on Your Confidence

In the face of such discouragement, Hebrews challenges us to have, and to act on, confidence in Christ. After all, Jesus has fully identified with us (2:14); mediated a liberating new covenant (9:15); and called us into partnership (3:14) as members of God's household, which he heads (3:6). He has blazed a trail for us to follow (2:10) into God's very presence (6:20), and he will bring us safe to the end (9:28). All of this taken together leads our author to exclaim, in 10:19, "Brothers and sisters, we have confidence!"

Ah, but confidence only is as confidence does. After briefly summarizing Jesus' work in 10:19-21, our author delivered his bracing "Therefore!" Because we can trust Jesus' work on our behalf, there are some things we need to do (10:22-24)—and no one said it would always be easy.

First, we must "draw near" to God. If there is one message in the entire book, this is it. At key moments all along (4:16; 7:19; 10:22), the author has been urging us to "draw near" to God. This is the point of the whole venture. Of what use would the best theology or the holiest life be if they did not bring us close to our Source (2:11)? It is all about relationship, about knowing God in an intimate and responsive way (8:10-12). This is what Jesus offers: closeness to God. Nothing less will do.

Our relationship with God does not exist in a vacuum, however. It is incumbent on us to do the hard work of holding onto our faith, of staying the course (10:23), because we believe that God's promises are more reliable and lasting than the troubles and temptations of this world. Though we, like Hebrews' original readers, may feel like the ancient Israelites —tired of wandering in the wilderness (3:7–4:10)—we must not give in to the temptation to go back to "life before liberation." We must trust that the wilderness is not the whole story, that God's promises are reliable. We must carry on in faith and faithfulness.

We are, moreover, called to help one another, to encourage and motivate one another to the "love and . . . good works" that belong to life in Christ (10:24-25). There is no room in the biblical vision for the solitary Christian, for the "good person" living a "good life" apart from the community of faith. We need one another. Even if you, at this moment, don't feel a special need for others, others may need you. It is together that we nourish the vision of faith, together that we do its best works. "Networking" is as essential in living for God as it is in business.

Take a moment to think about a specific way your friends could "spur [you] on" (10:24, New International Version) to love and good deeds. Could you ask for them to do this? Do you think others might appreciate if you did it for them? As preacher Herbert O'Driscoll reportedly said, "God has given us five gifts for the journey: word, water, bread, wine, and one another." Let's be sure to receive and use them all.

The Fear Factor

Just when we are beginning to feel confident that if God is for us who can be against us (Romans 8:31), Hebrews brings us down to earth with a bump: The enemy is us. The one thing that can come between us and the love of God is our decision, and Hebrews doesn't mince words about it. "If we make the decision to sin after we receive the knowledge of the truth, there isn't a sacrifice for sins left any longer. There's only a scary expectation of judgment" (10:26-27a).

About the Scripture

The Day of the Lord

Hebrews 10:25 urges people to remain committed to the Christian community, "especially as you see the day drawing near." This day, which is also alluded to in the Old Testament passages quoted in verses 37 and 38, is the Day of the Lord. It is mentioned frequently by the prophets (for example, Isaiah 2:2-21; Joel 1–3; Amos 8:9-11; 9:9-12) and came to be widely anticipated by the time of Jesus.

On that "day" (or in that pivotal time), God would intervene in human affairs to abolish evil, restore Israel to faithfulness and to independence, and establish an ideal society under the leadership of the Messiah descended from King David. God's enemies, within and beyond Israel, would be destroyed, which is why the Day of the Lord is also known as the Day of Judgment.

Whenever times were particularly difficult (such as during the Roman occupation under which Jesus was born), people's eagerness for the Day of the Lord would peak, and they would look avidly for the Messiah, even though the prophets warned that no one would escape judgment at that time (Amos 5:18-24; Malachi 3:1-5). Jesus, near the end of his ministry, spoke of how difficult the Day of the Lord would be (Matthew 24–25; Mark 13).

Because Christians believed Jesus was the Messiah, the one who would bring in the Day of the Lord and rule from then on, they trusted that his departure was not final but that he would return, probably quite soon, to establish his reign on earth. Thus many places in the New Testament (such as 1 Corinthians 15:20-26; 1 Thessalonians 5:1-6; and James 5:7-8) mention "his coming" or "the day" as a source of hope and a reason to persevere in right living.

Ever since people started believing in a Day of the Lord, they have been trying to predict when and how it will happen. Jesus himself cautioned against this effort, saying that he himself didn't know, only God (Mark 13:32-33). Rather than debating over the details, we would do well to treat this concept as the Bible does—as a statement of trust in God and a reminder that our actions matter.

We need to be clear about what kind of sin is in view here. Hebrews is not talking about the daily slips and stumbles we all make. For those we can look to the guidance of our fellow Christians (10:24-25) and to Jesus' ongoing intercession on our behalf (7:25). What Hebrews is talking about is a much more serious issue but one that can sneak up on us when we fail to nurture and exercise our faith: turning away from God, especially by rejecting

Jesus. In 10:28-31, there are several allusions to the Old Testament, and they all concern idolatry, which is the worship of (or reliance on) false gods. Trusting something other than God, less than God. That is what "insults the Spirit of grace" and spits all over Jesus' offering for us (10:29).

If you have been raised to think of God as judgmental, or if you are in a period of struggle, it may be difficult for you to hear any good news in this passage. The author was not trying to frighten his readers just for the sake of browbeating them. He was afraid that they were in fairly immediate danger of missing out on the rewards of life in Christ, perhaps of giving up on him altogether. Hebrews was written to shock people into getting the big picture straight: No matter what's going on in the present, the future belongs to God. Jesus did the same in Matthew 10:28, saying, "Don't be afraid of those who kill the body but can't kill the soul. Instead, be afraid of the one who can destroy both body and soul in hell."

Our Scriptures show us a God who is both loving and upright, at once merciful and judging. Some churches play heavily on the judgmental aspect; others are only comfortable with a "gentle Jesus, meek and mild." How have you primarily understood God? Does your habitual vision seem adequate; or does it need to be fleshed out, maybe even changed? Has fear played a significant part in your religious experience; or have you been complacent, maybe even a little too much so? Has reading Hebrews made you feel more afraid or less? Take time to talk with someone you trust about your thoughts and feelings.

It is important in reading this section of Hebrews to hold it in context with the book as a whole. The overwhelming emotion the author seeks to evoke is confidence—confidence in the promises of God, in the work of Jesus on our behalf, and in our ability to walk the walk. However, the author was addressing people in an emotional situation, where they frequently suffered hostility and disgrace for their faith. So once he had spent the first few chapters of the book building up their confidence in Jesus, he began to work with their distress from the other side as well. There are bigger and more powerful things to fear than public opinion! When you consider the consequences of rejecting the God of time and eternity, your next-door neighbor's raised eyebrows suddenly don't seem so important anymore.

Still, fear and shame are potent weapons, so Hebrews uses them, if devastatingly, also sparingly. The warnings are painful, but they are always bracketed by strong encouragement and expressions of trust in the readers. What the author wanted to inspire was not anxiety but the kind of confidence that can stand up to hardship and act boldly in faith. "[Don't] be lazy," he urged in 6:12, "but follow the example of the ones who inherit the promises through faith and patience." He made the same point in Chapter 10: "You need to endure so that you can receive the promises after you do God's will" (verse 36).

Live Up to Your Own Example

Lest his readers worry that they'd been getting the Christian life altogether wrong, the author urged them to remember and to live up to their own example. During an earlier period of intense persecution, they had stood up to "an enormous amount of pressure" (10:32) with remarkable courage and grace. Whether it was public humiliation, the imprisonment of Christian friends, or the pillaging of their homes, they had been able to weather the mistreatment by keeping before their eyes the fact that they had "better and [more] lasting possessions" than anything they were losing (10:34). This perspective allowed them to stand in open solidarity with one another, courageously and compassionately helping one another through that terrible time.

Then something seemed to change. Perhaps it was the sandpaper effect of continuous low-grade hostility or the early signs of another flare-up of persecution. Perhaps it was other troubles and the dawning realization that coming to Christ doesn't miraculously solve life's problems. Whatever the cause, they were losing heart for the Christian life, drifting away from the church, neglecting their spiritual lives and the needs of others. Their confidence and vitality had ebbed. "You need to endure," urged the author, "so that you can receive the promises after you do God's will" (10:36). Think about all you've endured and all you've accomplished. Don't throw it all away!

Old Testament Roots of Hebrews 10:19-39

Hebrews 10:22: Our heart and conscience have been cleansed so that we can approach God.	*Ezekiel 36:25-28*: God will cleanse disobedient Israel so that they can live as God's people.
Hebrews 10:26: There is no atonement for knowing, willful sin.	*Numbers 15:30-31*: High-handed rebellion is grounds for expulsion from the community.
Hebrews 10:27: The fire of judgment will consume God's opponents.	*Isaiah 26:10-11*: When God judges earth, let the fire for God's adversaries also consume unjust Israelites.
Hebrews 10:28: Death penalty for (properly witnessed) rejection of the law of Moses; this penalty is "without mercy."	*Deuteronomy 17:2-7*: Idolatry (properly witnessed) is punishable by death; this is without mercy in the case of idolatry (Deuteronomy 13:8).
Hebrews 10:29: Jesus' blood of the [new] covenant	*Exodus 24:8*: Animal blood institutes Moses' covenant.
Hebrews 10:30: "Judgment is mine, I will pay people back; the Lord will judge his people."	*Deuteronomy 32:35-36 (LXX)*: "In the day of vengeance I will recompense. For the Lord shall judge his people."
Hebrews 10:31: "It's scary to fall into the hands of the living God!"	*Deuteronomy 32:39-41*: No one can deliver from God's hand; it wields sword of judgment on enemies.
Hebrews 10:37-38: In a little while he is coming. God's righteous live by faith, but he is displeased with those who shrink back.	*Isaiah 26:20-21*: Israel had to wait "a little while" through difficult times for God to act. *Habakkuk 2:3-4 (LXX)*: [God's judgment] is surely coming; *verse 4 LXX* reads: "If he should draw back, my soul has no pleasure in him: but the just shall live by my faith."

Live the Story

The writer of Hebrews was convinced that once redeemed, we are able to walk on Jesus' path to the glorious completion of God's promise; but sometimes it's hard to be motivated by something far ahead.

Still, many people will attest that faith is its own reward. The courage and grace it gives make life better here and now, even before the promised eternal fulfillment. However, faith can be hard to sustain through a lifetime of challenges and distractions. What things particularly challenge your faith right now?

To help place things in perspective, make yourself a "faith timeline" on a large sheet of paper. Draw a line horizontally across the middle of the page. Place the year of your birth at one end, the current year at the other. Mark off the line in five- or ten-year increments. Let the dates remind you of significant events in your life and in the world. Note these things at appropriate places below the line. Above the line, start making date-connected notes about your faith journey. Think about how you thought of God as a child and how that changed as you matured. Can you recall specific spiritual experiences or milestones? Are there questions or problems you have wrestled with? When has God been most real to you? seemed most distant? When have you felt most confident you were doing God's will or serving God most effectively?

When you have filled in all you can think of (this may take several sessions over a number of days), look at the whole picture. How has your faith life intertwined with the events of your everyday story and with what's happening in the wider world? Can you see how God has sustained and guided you?

In prayer, place the whole story before God. Tell God how you feel about it. Ask God to show you anything you need to notice. Now set your present issues in the context of the ongoing story, and listen for what the Spirit may wish to say to you about them. Is there any support you need to seek or to offer others in order to faithfully carry on?

5.

Seeing the Unseen

Hebrews 11

Claim Your Story

Anyone who spends time in a church is sure to be exhorted, sooner or later, to have faith. Maybe you've been told to have faith in Jesus for salvation, or to have faith that God is doing something through your hardship, or to believe that all things are possible for faith. Just what is faith, anyway? Can you be sure that you have it, have enough of it, or are having faith in the right things?

What are some of the things you have been told, or have thought, about faith? Have you wondered or worried at all about your faith?

If you remember, with tears in your eyes, the day the last of the Chilean miners came safely to the surface after 70 days underground, then you understand faith. For many weeks after the cave-in, people on the surface worked frantically to devise and build a rescue shaft, while others found ways to provide supplies to the trapped miners. Underground, shift supervisor Luis Urzua organized and encouraged his men to survive their physical and their psychological danger.

Although the chances of successful rescue seemed remote, especially in the two long weeks before they were even located, nobody within or outside the mine gave up, but kept working toward a better outcome. Astonishingly, although it took a long time, every last miner was eventually brought safely to the surface, health and sanity intact.

Enter the Bible Story

Look at What Faith Can Do

The faith of which Hebrews speaks is this same kind of refusal to let go of an unseen and often enough improbable outcome. Although the world as it is presses in on us daily, people of faith dare to believe in—and, more importantly, to act upon—the world that God intends.

The author of Hebrews was speaking to people who were under fire for their faith, people whose family, friends, and neighbors considered Christianity a cult and whose own memories drew them back to the Judaism of their childhood. It would have been so easy to give up on Jesus. Indeed, some of them had begun to draw away from the church, missing services (10:25). Perhaps they hoped to fade into the woodwork in between the church and the synagogue, attending neither.

This still happens. We may not be persecuted for our faith, but plenty of people today feel a conflict between the worlds of biblical faith and of modernity. They drift quietly away from church, taking their questions and their aspirations with them to wither in silence.

Hebrews challenges us to a bolder approach. Faith has never been easy, trusting God never the obvious choice. From Abel who believed that not just any old offering would do and thus gave the richest and best parts of his first returns, down to the heroes of the Maccabean revolt who refused to blend into the pagan background, Hebrews 11 marshals a huge list of people who chose to believe that what they could not see was not only more vital but also more reliable than what they could see.

Hebrews doesn't go into detail. It assumes readers will be familiar with the stories. More important in any case is the sheer volume of examples. You are not the first to have to live by faith, insisted the author. You're part of a long and courageous line. Anything you are going through has already been experienced and more besides. Those people were not discouraged. Neither should you be. Look at what faith can do!

A Way of Seeing

First, faith gives us a way of seeing the world, of framing our experience. "By faith we understand that the universe has been created by a word from God," began our author (11:3), thus setting our entire existence within the context of God's care. Contrary to what many seem to think, this vision is not at odds with scientific understanding; it simply exists independently of it. Science neither requires nor refutes a creating God. That is not a question science can answer. However, when faith answers that there is a God behind the universe and that this God is going somewhere with us, it changes everything.

Consider the Chilean miners. For two weeks they had no contact with the outside world. After the first few days or a week, they must have wondered whether anybody was still looking urgently for them. After all, it is highly unusual for anyone to survive more than a few days in such a situation. The men had portioned out their food and water to last as long as possible; but even at a mere teaspoon of tuna a day, the food ran out without a sign that anyone knew they were alive. They surely must have thought they were dead men walking.

Then, the day after the food ran out, contact was established. From that time, they knew that the world knew they were alive. They knew a rescue effort was underway. They still had to live with darkness, hunger, heat, fear, and deprivation; but they knew that help was coming. That assurance made all the difference.

In the same way, for us, trusting that God is at work behind the world makes all the difference. Whether we are venturing into unknown territory like Abraham, going up against overwhelming odds like Gideon, or speaking an unpopular truth like the prophet Jeremiah, we need to know that something bigger and more reliable than our own little selves is behind us. It is this that powers people of faith to do such extraordinary things. We know we are not alone.

Real People, Real World

It is tempting for us to look at the heroes of faith and think, "Oh, well, they were different." The Bible makes it quite clear that they were not. Abraham did not know that people 4,000 years later would be revering his

Across the Testaments

Old Testament Roots of Hebrews 11

Hebrews 11:3: The universe has been created by a word from God.	*Genesis 1*: God speaks the universe into existence (also Psalm 33:6, 9).
Hebrews 11:4: Abel offered a better sacrifice than Cain.	*Genesis 4:3-5*: Abel's sacrifice approved over Cain's
Hebrews 11:5: Enoch pleased God and bypassed death.	*Genesis 5:24*: Enoch walked with God, and God took him (also Sirach 44:16).
Hebrews 11:7: Noah built an ark.	*Genesis 6:11-22*: Noah builds an ark.
Hebrews 11:8: Abraham set out in obedience to God's call.	*Genesis 12:1-4*: Abram (later called Abraham) sets out when God calls.
Hebrews 11:9: Abraham lived as a foreigner in the Promised Land.	*Genesis 20:1; 23:4*: Abraham is a resident alien in Canaan.
Hebrews 11:9: Isaac and Jacob also lived in tents [as temporary residents].	*Genesis 35:27*: Jacob, like Abraham and Isaac, was a resident alien at Hebron.
Hebrews 11:11: Sarah, old and barren, received a child by faith.	*Genesis 18:9-15; 21:1-2*: Despite initial disbelief, Sarah bears a son.
Hebrews 11:12: Abraham's descendants uncountable as stars, sand	*Genesis 22:17*: God promises Abraham offspring as numerous as stars and sand. [This core promise is repeated many times in Genesis, Exodus, and Deuteronomy; also Sirach 44:21.]
Hebrews 11:13: They saw the promises from a distance and welcomed them.	*Deuteronomy 3:23-27; 34:1-4*: Moses sees the Promised Land but cannot enter.
Hebrews 11:13: The faithful all knew they were strangers on earth.	*1 Chronicles 29:15*: David/Israelites, like their ancestors, are transients on earth. Psalm 39:12: God's passing guests

Hebrews 11:16: God is the God of these faithful ones.	*Exodus 3:6, 15; 4:5* (and many other places): God of Abraham, Isaac, Jacob
Hebrews 11:17: Abraham offered Isaac, his only [acknowledged] son.	*Genesis 22:1-19*: God tests Abraham by asking him to sacrifice Isaac.
Hebrews 11:18: It was through Isaac that descendants were promised.	*Genesis 21:12*: It is through Isaac you shall have the promised descendants.
Hebrews 11:20: Isaac blessed Jacob and Esau concerning their future.	*Genesis 27:28-29, 39-40*: Isaac blesses Jacob and Esau, speaks of their future.
Hebrews 11:21: Jacob blessed Joseph's sons.	*Genesis 48*: Jacob blesses Joseph's sons.
Hebrews 11:22: Joseph, confident of eventual exodus, gives burial instructions.	*Genesis 50:24-25*: Joseph's last words. [These instructions were obeyed. See Exodus 13:19.]
Hebrews 11:23: Moses' parents hid him.	*Exodus 2:1-4*: Moses' parents hide him.
Hebrews 11:23: Moses' parents were unafraid of the king's orders.	*Exodus 1:22*: The Pharaoh (king) ordered all male Hebrew infants killed.
Hebrews 11:24: Moses refused royal identity and privilege.	*Exodus 2:11-12*: Moses identified with enslaved Hebrews, not Egyptian court.
Hebrews 11:27: Moses left Egypt.	*Exodus 12:50-51*: Moses led the Israelites out of Egypt.
Hebrews 11:28: Moses kept the Passover.	*Exodus 12:21-30*: Moses and the Israelites observe the first Passover.
Hebrews 11:29: They crossed the Red Sea.	*Exodus 14*: Israelites cross the Red Sea.
Hebrews 11:30: Jericho's walls fell.	*Joshua 6:1-20*: Jericho is taken.
Hebrews 11:31: Rahab's life was spared because she welcomed the spies.	*Joshua 2:1-16*: Rahab shelters the spies. *Joshua 6:21-25*: Rahab's life is spared.
Hebrews 11:32: Gideon	*Judges 6–7*: Gideon routs Midianites.

Hebrews 11:32: Barak	*Judges 4*: Deborah and Barak defeat Sisera.
Hebrews 11:32: Samson	*Judges 13–16*: Samson kills Philistines.
Hebrews 11:32: Jephthah	*Judges 11*: Jephthah beats Ammonites.
Hebrews 11:32: David	*1 Samuel 16:1–1 Kings 2:11*: David's rise and reign; Israel's greatest king
Hebrews 11:32: Samuel and the prophets	*1 Samuel 1:1–25:1*: Samuel *1 Kings 17–19, 21; 2 Kings 1–2*: Elijah *2 Kings 4:1–8:15*: Elisha *Books of Isaiah through Malachi*
Hebrews 11:33: Shut lions' mouths	*Daniel 6*: In the lions' den
Hebrews 11:34: Quenched fires	*Daniel 3*: In the fiery furnace
Hebrews 11:34: Escaped the sword	*1 King 19:1-3*: Elijah escapes.
Hebrews 11:35: Women received loved ones back from the dead.	*1 Kings 17:17-24*: A widow's son raised *2 Kings 4:17-37*: Shunammite's son lives.
Hebrews 11:35: Others refused deliverance in hope of a better resurrection.	*2 Maccabees 6:18–7:42*: Eleazar and seven brothers die rather than eat pork.
Hebrews 11:36: Mocking, flogging, imprisonment	*Jeremiah 20:2; 37:15; 38:6*: Jeremiah's sufferings for speaking the truth
Hebrews 11:37: Stoned to death	*2 Chronicles 24:20-21*: Zechariah stoned for calling nation to account.
Hebrews 11:37: Cut in two	An old tradition says King Manasseh (*2 Kings 21:16*) killed Isaiah this way.
Hebrews 11:38: Deserts, mountains, caves, and holes in the ground	*1 Samuel 23:15–24:3*: David a fugitive *1 Kings 18:4; 19:9*: Prophets in caves

example. Moses did not grow up thinking he would be a prophet and hero of the Jewish nation. While their stories may have been embroidered by the time they found their way into the Bible, we can still see real human beings living real lives in the real world and reacting much as you or I would to the circumstances in which they found themselves.

There are few plaster saints in the Bible; even the greatest heroes are portrayed warts and all and are sometimes shown to fail dramatically. This is important because the Bible is calling us to follow their example. We can only be responsible to do what they did if they're the same kind of human beings that we are.

And they are. As Hebrews takes us on a whirlwind tour of Bible history, it is talking about people just like us. Abraham was a coward (Genesis 20:11); Sarah snickered at God's promise (Genesis 18:12); Moses desperately tried to evade his calling (Exodus 3:11, 13; 4:1, 10, 13); and Jacob cheated his brother, Esau (Genesis 25:29-34). Rahab was a prostitute, and it seems some of the Israelite spies may have enjoyed her services (Joshua 2:1). Jephthah made a stupid promise that cost his daughter's life (Judges 11:30-39). David committed adultery and murder (2 Samuel 11). The list could go on. Yet these are all cited as examples of faith, because in spite of their all-too-human failings, they kept on reaching toward the vision of God's future.

It is not only the personal failings of our faith forebears that the Bible chronicles. They also experienced the whole range of the human condition, including many situations that are commonly held to render people disadvantaged or even powerless.

Jacob (Genesis 25:25-26), Joseph (Genesis 35:23-26), and David (1 Samuel 16:6-13) were younger sons in a society where wealth and authority went to the eldest. Moses was born into slavery (Exodus 1:8–2:2), and Joseph was sold into it (Genesis 37:12-28). Abraham spent much of his life as a resident alien dependent on the good graces of local people and rulers (Genesis 20:1, 23:4). Daniel and his friends were deported to a foreign country (Daniel 1:1-7). Joseph (Genesis 41:37–44:17) and David (2 Samuel 11-12) faced the temptations of power. Daunting military odds confronted the people many times (Numbers 13:31; Joshua 11:1-5; Judges

4:3), as well as discouraging circumstances following Israel's defeat and exile (Ezra 4:4-5; Nehemiah 1:1-3). Prophets often encountered hostility and even accusations of treason because their messages were unwelcome (1 Kings 21:17-20; Jeremiah 37:12-16; 38:4; Amos 7:10).

Yet God's people soldiered on. Faith has always had to make its way in the grit of the real world.

Taking the Long View

What kept—and keeps—people of faith going was their trust that, in the end, God is in charge and God has a plan. Many of the earlier heroes grasped only a small part of that plan: Abraham hoped for family and land, Moses for freedom and a homeland for his people. As time passed, the vision grew. By the time David assumed the throne, the prospect included a royal dynasty (1 Chronicles 17:1-15), which became the basis for Israel's hope in a Messiah.

Early Christians such as the apostle Paul (Romans 1:16; Galatians 3:28) and the writer of Hebrews came to see that in Jesus, God was bringing to fruition the whole of his people's story. God was crowning the sum of it with something they were just beginning to glimpse: the spiritual salvation of every human being, whether Jewish or not, who desired to come to God. This is what the author meant in Hebrews 11:40, when he wrapped up his inspiring inventory by stating, "God provided something better for us so they wouldn't be made perfect without us." The faith of the earlier heroes was based on an incomplete vision. That vision is completed ("made perfect") when Jesus invites the whole world to draw near to God.

Today, people of faith continue to hear and bravely respond to the Spirit's call into ever more inclusive visions so that all people and all of creation can flourish as God intended from the beginning (Genesis 1:31). The first Christians expected Jesus to return quite soon to establish God's reign on earth (Hebrews 10:25b). Some 2,000 years later, we must accept that at least some of the responsibility is ours. We must ask what God is calling us to do for the well-being of the world God loves.

We have a rich legacy. Numberless people of faith who preceded us (a whole great "cloud of witnesses," as Hebrews 12:1 states) assure us that our faith is not in vain. We may not see the whole picture even yet; but we trust that God is working out something more wonderful than we can imagine (Ephesians 3:20), not only for us personally but for all of humanity. Our wholeness, individually and as a human race, is God's ultimate plan. Although we may not see much evidence of that sometimes, here on the ground, we hold onto the conviction and work toward it persistently.

Live the Story

Karen Armstrong, in her book *The Spiral Staircase*, notes that religion (like faith) is "not about accepting twenty impossible propositions before breakfast but about doing things that change you." Abraham got up and left home. Moses turned his back on royal privilege. Jesus laid down his life. In doing these things, they changed not only their own lives but the world. They moved us a step closer to God's desire.

Their models of faithfulness can help us live worthy lives and give us hope to reach the final goal that they saw only "from a distance" (Hebrews 11:13). Thus, we are called to continue that journey. When we're immersed in the details of our daily lives, it can be easy to forget that. We tend to let our vision shrink down to the size of our most pressing momentary concerns. Sometimes it takes a crisis to remind us that life is about so much more than the daily grind or our personal pleasure. What sort of outcome do you think God wants for you? for those around you?

Read back over Hebrews 11 prayerfully, inviting God to draw one of these people of faith to your attention. Read that person's story in the Old Testament (find where in the *Across the Testaments* sidebar), and ponder how their story resonates with your own. What could you learn from this faith ancestor about growing into God's vision?

Write down a few things that help you walk in faith and a few things that hinder you. Now, what one small thing can you do today, this week, to take responsibility for growing in your active loyalty to God's vision for your life and the world? Write it down. Do it!

6.

Staying the Course With Jesus

Hebrews 12–13

Claim Your Story

When I was in high school music, the bandmaster insisted that his students drill scales. Major scales, minor scales, chromatic scales, all the way around the circle of fifths—we had to be able to play them all, fast and accurately. Sitting in my other classes, anytime I wasn't actively taking notes, I'd hold my pen as if it were my instrument and practice my scales. I haven't picked up a saxophone in over 20 years; but to this day, I can "play" those scales on a pen.

What my bandmaster knew was that training our fingers on the scales around which music is built would prepare us to pick up even a difficult piece and learn to play it well. In the same way, cross-country runners do wind sprints, short all-out dashes repeated over and over until the legs and lungs plead for mercy, as a way of building capacity for long-distance runs.

Whether you're training for the Olympics or helping your child learn to read, you know that working hard at the basics is what lays the foundation for long-term success.

Enter the Bible Story

To Run Freely in Faith

The closing pages of Hebrews sketch out for us basic attitudes and practices on which to ground a well-lived Christian life. Chapter 12 opens by comparing faith to a race, a race for which we must strip ourselves of entanglements and run with determination, focused on the goal of Christ-likeness.

This is a countercultural message. Our society dangles all kinds of enticements before our eyes, encouraging us to seek pleasure rather than making the effort to build character and community. Self-care and enjoyment are not incompatible with solid faithfulness. Remember that Jesus offered his followers rest as well as a cross (Matthew 11:28; 16:24). However, grounding our lives on the sand of momentary pleasure will fail us (Matthew 7:24-27). The sometimes grueling effort of a disciplined life of faith, on the other hand, offers solid returns of peace and right living (Hebrews 12:11).

Consider what extra baggage or outright sin (12:1) is compromising your discipleship at this moment. What would it take to strip that away? How would it feel to be running more freely in faith?

Hard Training

Earlier in Hebrews (2:10), the author spoke of Jesus being made perfect, or fitted for his redemptive task, by what he suffered. In 12:5-11, he spoke of the role of suffering in our lives. We can all attest that we have grown and matured through hard times: Difficulties challenge us to grow up, dig deeper, and work harder to be our best and bravest selves. However, does God actually bring suffering upon us for the purpose of correction —even punishment—as Hebrews says? Such a theology easily turns God into an abuser and makes it easier for humans to abuse one another.

Jesus, while he didn't reject the Bible's assumption that God can use suffering as punishment, did challenge the blanket application of it. When his disciples wondered whether a man was born blind because of his parents' sin or his own, Jesus said it was neither but "so that God's mighty works might be displayed in him" (John 9:2-3).

Jesus also acknowledged that some misfortunes are simply random events (Luke13:4-5a). God does not micro-manage everything that happens in this world. That would turn us into puppets. However, if we choose to receive difficulties as coming to us from or through the wise and loving hands of God, then we are best positioned to grow in grace. This trusting approach bolsters our happiness and confidence as well. The God who loves us does not wish to see us discouraged or embittered (Hebrews 12:3, 15).

It is up to us, however, not only to adopt an attitude that will allow us to profit from our experiences but also to avoid unnecessary pitfalls. A certain amount of bruising and strain comes with any training regimen, and certainly with the arduous business of life; but the wise athlete takes care to prevent serious injury. The Book of Hebrews gives us many tips on preventing career-ending faith injuries.

When the author urged his readers to "make straight paths for your feet" (12:13), he probably had in mind things such as clearing away the clutter of unorthodoxy (13:9); getting rid of any sins we may be harboring (12:1); meditating on Jesus (12:2) and the example of others (11:4-38, 13:7); placing ourselves in regular contact with the faith community (10:25); accepting the guidance of church leaders (13:17); recalling our own times of strength and the perspective we had then (10:32-36); letting the word of God search and correct us (4:12-13); living gratefully, generously, and according to our convictions (12:14-16, 13:1-18); and keeping our hearts open to God (3:12-13; 12:25). These choices, made day by day, over and over again, like running laps, will keep us strong, hopeful, resilient, and growing in our faith, a credit to the one who saves us.

The consequences of failing to stay in shape were sadly illustrated by Esau, whose inability to see past the difficulty of the moment (Hebrews 12:16; Genesis 25:32) cost him the double inheritance and place of leadership that should have been his. Although we do not like to think of God turning anyone away, Hebrews warns us that some choices cannot be undone. Our relationship with Christ and our life of faith must be worked at, not treated as expendable.

Making the Choice

By way of encouragement, Hebrews once again evokes the contrast between the forbidding, unapproachable God of Sinai and our joyous communion with God in the new covenant community (12:18-24). Though Jesus was tortured and executed as an enemy of the state, his blood does not cry out for justice or vengeance like Abel's (Hebrews 12:24). Instead, by his gracious self-giving, his blood has become the means of our reconciliation with God and one another.

Across the Testaments

Old Testament Roots of Hebrews 12–13

Hebrews 12:2: Jesus sat down at the right hand of God's throne.	*Psalm 110:1*: "The LORD says to my lord, 'Sit at my right hand.'"
Hebrews 12:5-6: Don't make light of or be discouraged by God's discipline. God corrects those he loves.	*Proverbs 3:11-12*: Don't make light of or be discouraged by God's discipline. God corrects those he loves.
Hebrews 12:7: God is treating you like his own children when he disciplines you.	*Deuteronomy 8:5*: As a parent disciplines a child, so God disciplines you.
Hebrews 12:12: Strengthen your drooping hands and weak knees.	*Isaiah 35:3-4*: Strengthen your weak hands, knees. God is coming to save you!
Hebrews 12:13: Make straight paths so as not to be further lamed.	*Proverbs 4:26:* Keep straight paths so all your ways will be sure. (See also Isaiah 40:3.)
Hebrews 12:14: Pursue peace and holiness.	*Psalm 34:14*: Do good and pursue peace.
Hebrews 12:14: No one will see the Lord without holiness.	*Psalm 15:1-2*: Who may abide in God's presence? Those who do what is right.
Hebrews 12:15: Make sure no root of bitterness grows up that might cause trouble and pollute people.	*Deuteronomy 29:18*: Some of your hearts may be turning to other gods, a bitter root sprouting poisonous growth.
Hebrews 12:16: Esau sold his inheritance.	*Genesis 25:29-34*: Esau sells birthright.
Hebrews 12:17: Esau couldn't change the outcome despite his tears.	*Genesis 27:30-38*: Esau begs in vain for his lost blessing.
Hebrews 12:18-19: Burning fire, darkness, shadow, whirlwind, trumpet blast, terror; the people begged that God not speak directly to them.	*Exodus 19:16-19; 20:18-21*: When the first covenant was established at Sinai, the sights and sounds were so terrifying the people begged God to speak only to Moses, not them.

Hebrews 12:20: If even a wild animal touches the mountain it shall be stoned.	*Exodus 19:12-13*: No human or animal shall touch the mountain and live.
Hebrews 12:21: Even Moses was terrified by the sight and shook.	No record that Moses feared the sight, but he did fear God's rejection for the people's disobedience: *Deuteronomy 9:19*.
Hebrews 12:23: You have come to the assembly of the firstborn.	*Numbers 3:12-13*: The Levites (priestly tribe) belong to God on behalf of all first-borns: holy.
Hebrews 12:23: You've come to God, judge of all, and to righteous spirits made perfect.	*Genesis 18:25*: The Judge of all the earth will do right, not destroy innocent with guilty.
Hebrews 12:24: Jesus' blood speaks a better word than Abel's.	*Genesis 4:10*: Blood of murdered Abel cries out to God from the ground.
Hebrews 12:26: God's voice shook the earth.	Exodus 19:18: Mount Sinai shook (and Judges 5:5; Psalm 29:3-9; Psalm 68:8; Psalm 77:18).
Hebrews 12:26: I will again shake not just the earth but the heavens.	*Haggai 2:6, 21-23*: I will again shake the heavens and earth [and make all things right].
Hebrews 12:29: Our God is a consuming fire.	*Exodus 24:17*: God appeared on Sinai like a devouring fire. (See also Deuteronomy 4:24; 9:3; Isaiah 33:14; God is like a fire in purity, power, and judgment.)
Hebrews 13:2: Some have hosted angels without knowing it.	*Genesis 18:1-8, 19:1-3*: Abraham and Lot host divine messengers.
Hebrews 13:5: God has promised never to abandon us.	*Deuteronomy 31:6, 8*: God will not abandon Israel.
Hebrews 13:6: God is my helper, I won't fear. What can mere humans do to me?	*Psalm 118:6:* With the Lord on my side, I do not fear: what can mortals do to me?

Hebrews 13:9: It is good to be strengthened by grace, not food, which has not helped.	*Leviticus 11:1-23*: "Clean" and "unclean" foods (sample portion of Jewish dietary law)
Hebrews 13:10: We have an altar from which priests in the tent have no right to eat.	*Leviticus 6:14-18; 7:1-6*: Jewish priests burned a certain part of sacrifices, ate the rest.
Hebrews 13:11: Once the blood is offered, the body is burned outside the camp.	*Leviticus 16:27*: On Day of Atonement, after blood is offered, carcass burned outside camp.
Hebrews 13:15: Let's continually offer up a sacrifice of praise.	*Leviticus 7:11-12*: Instructions for the thanksgiving (LXX "praise") offering (a special voluntary gift). (See also Psalm 50:14, 23; Psalm 107:22.)
Hebrews 13:15: Our praise sacrifice is the fruit of lips that confess Jesus' name.	*Hosea 14:2*: Return to God with the fruit of your lips: words of repentance.
Hebrews 13:17: Your leaders watch over you as people who will be held responsible.	*Ezekiel 3:17-21*: God makes the prophet accountable for guarding and warning people.
Hebrews 13:20: God brought back from death the great shepherd of the sheep.	*LXX Isaiah 63:11-12* reads: "He that brought up from the sea the shepherd of the sheep . . . who led Moses with his right hand."
Hebrews 13:20: Jesus is the great shepherd of the sheep.	*Ezekiel 34:23*: I will set up over them one shepherd, [a descendant of] my servant David. (See also Isaiah 40:11.)
Hebrews 13:20: We have an eternal covenant established by Jesus' blood.	*Exodus 24:8*: Sinai covenant established by blood. (See also Zechariah 9:11.)
Hebrews 13:20: Eternal covenant	*Isaiah 55:3*: I will make with you an everlasting covenant. (See also Jeremiah 32:40; Ezekiel 37:26.)

But it doesn't just happen. We must choose to accept those renewed relationships and to live in a manner worthy of them. Writing to people who were drifting away from Christianity under the threat of persecution, the author of Hebrews issued a stern warning alongside his luminous hope: Yes, an unshakeable new creation is coming; and you are invited to be part of it. But do not think you will be left standing if you fail to anchor in Christ (12:25-29).

He then sketched out what it means to walk with Jesus day to day—the scales and wind sprints of Christian life. Strikingly, this is a life in community: "Keep loving each other like family. Don't neglect to open up your homes to guests. . . . Remember prisoners as if you were in prison with them, and people who are mistreated as if you were in their place" (13:1-3).

Just as Jesus identified and sympathized with us, we are to identify and sympathize with one another. For the persecuted first-century church, this took some courage. It would have been natural for people to distance themselves from imprisoned or harassed fellow Christians in order to avoid suffering similar trouble. Hebrews, however, like the New Testament in general, recognizes no separation among Christians. When one suffers, all suffer (1 Corinthians 12:26). We all must support and care for one another.

Indeed, our care and welcome are to be extended even to strangers. The word used for "hospitality" in 13:2 does not refer only to invited guests but to anyone needing a place to stay. How does this speak to your attitude to newcomers to your country? In the face of an often panicky and hostile public, Christians are called to a witness of compassion and confident bridge-building.

We are also summoned to a high moral standard. In contrast to the lax sexual norms of the first century (and our own), Hebrews upholds the biblical standard of marital fidelity and of confining sex to the marriage relationship (13:4). Think about your sexual history. How has your exercise of your sexuality enhanced your life and that of your partner(s)? Do you have any regrets? What sexual blessings, challenges, and opportunities confront you now?

Hebrews also warns against the perennial idol of money. A useful and necessary tool, it makes a bad substitute for God. As 1 Timothy 6:10 also points out, it is not money itself that is the problem but our attachment to it. When we desire and rely on it, giving it power in our lives, it leads us into all kinds of trouble. Yet unlike God, money cannot be counted on never to abandon us. It comes and goes (Hebrews 13:5). Our lives need to be founded on deeper things.

Ponder your relationship with money. Has the search for financial security led you to transgress other values? Does your use of your resources reflect your beliefs about what God values most? Is money a source of anxiety or conflict in your home? What are the reasons for that? Offer a prayer to God to guide you into a more wholesome relationship with this basic resource.

Outside the Camp

Modern Christians often forget that Christianity spent its first several centuries as a marginalized minority faith. When the author of Hebrews cautioned his readers not to get carried away by the "many strange teachings out there" (13:9), he may well have been referring to Jewish teachings that most people would have considered much less strange than his own.

Alternatively, he might have been referring to the proliferation of other cults and new religions that flourished at the time. Just as Christians today are often drawn to fuzzy New Age thinking about angels, crystals, "manifesting" good fortune, and so on, Christians from the beginning have been curious about and inclined to dabble in the teachings and practices of other faiths and pseudo-faiths.

Hebrews reminds us to strengthen our hearts with the assurance of God's grace and to stay the course with Jesus even when it's difficult. Jesus offers something much better than comforting angel wings or the illusion of control over our circumstances. He offers confident access to the living God, a wholesome life that blesses us and those around us, and the assurance of eternal life in God's presence. Even if, at times in this life, we share the rejection of the one who was crucified outside the city walls (like the

Into the Camp and Back Out

When the Roman emperor Constantine adopted Christianity in A.D. 312, the young faith not only became legal, it enjoyed imperial favor and quickly ascended to a position of dominance in what became the Roman Empire. Many thoughtful Christians see this as having been an unhealthy development. Scriptures originally written to help people struggling on the margins of society have a different ring when read by people in places of privilege. Certainly the opportunities and the temptations of power changed the course of Christian (and world) history. Now that Christianity is again becoming one voice among many, what difficulties and possibilities can you see for the followers of Jesus?

animals sacrificed for the people's sin and then burned outside the camp on the Day of Atonement [Leviticus 16:27]), that is an abuse we can feel honored to share.

Whether in good times or bad, Hebrews reminds us to offer our best to God: praise for God's nature and work, a life of doing good, and generosity (13:15-16). These are the heart of authentic Christian worship, sacrifices that never lose their currency.

Hebrews closes with personal greetings and requests and a beautiful benediction (13:20-21). This final blessing repeats two of the book's main themes: the eternal covenant in Jesus' blood and the desire for the readers to come to maturity as Christians. However, the theme of Jesus as high priest completely disappears, replaced by the picture of Jesus as shepherd. In language that looks back to Isaiah's description of an earlier shepherd, Moses, Jesus is the long-awaited "great shepherd" on whose care we can rely now and forever.

Live the Story

Well! It's been quite a journey. We have explored the sometimes-exotic world of first-century Jewish Christians and discovered connections to our own. In this journey, we have been in company with Jesus. We have pondered his character and work, and we have considered the implications these have for our lives. Take a moment now to think about all you have learned from Hebrews. What has been most important for you?

Reread the blessing (13:20-21). Notice what it says about God, about Jesus, about our hope, and about our life. Write a prayer of your own, lifting up what has become important for you about God or Jesus and expressing your greatest desire in response. Put this prayer where you will see it, and pray it daily for the next week. Praying persistently for the realization of God's will in our lives is a key aspect of staying the course with Jesus.

What daily actions can you take to build your capacity to do what you are praying for? Keep playing those scales, and you will discover the wonderful music you can make in company with Christ.

Leader Guide

People often view the Bible as a maze of obscure people, places, and events from centuries ago and struggle to relate it to their daily lives. Immersion invites us to experience the Bible as a record of God's loving revelation to humankind. These studies recognize our emotional, spiritual, and intellectual needs and welcome us into the Bible story and into deeper faith.

As leader of an Immersion group, you will help participants to encounter the Word of God and the God of the Word that will lead to new creation in Christ. You do not have to be an expert to lead; in fact, you will participate with your group in listening to and applying God's life-transforming Word to your lives. You and your group will explore the building blocks of the Christian faith through key stories, people, ideas, and teachings in every book of the Bible. You will also explore the bridges and points of connection between the Old and New Testaments.

Choosing and Using the Bible

The central goal of Immersion is engaging the members of your group with the Bible in a way that informs their minds, forms their hearts, and transforms the way they live out their Christian faith. Participants will need this study book and a Bible. Immersion is an excellent accompaniment to the Common English Bible (CEB). It shares with the CEB four common aims: clarity of language, faith in the Bible's power to transform lives, the emotional expectation that people will find the love of God, and the rational expectation that people will find the knowledge of God.

Other recommended study Bibles include *The New Interpreter's Study Bible* (NRSV), *The New Oxford Annotated Study Bible* (NRSV), *The HarperCollins Study Bible* (NRSV), the *NIV and TNIV Study Bibles*, and the *Archaeological Study Bible* (NIV). Encourage participants to use more than one translation. *The Message: The Bible in Contemporary Language* is a modern paraphrase of the Bible, based on the original languages. Eugene H. Peterson has created a masterful presentation of the Scripture text, which is best used alongside rather than in place of the CEB or another primary English translation.

One of the most reliable interpreters of the Bible's meaning is the Bible itself. Invite participants first of all to allow Scripture to have its say. Pay attention to context. Ask questions of the text. Read every passage with curiosity, always seeking to answer the basic Who? What? Where? When? and Why? questions.

Bible study groups should also have handy essential reference resources in case someone wants more information or needs clarification on specific words, terms, concepts, places, or people mentioned in the Bible. A Bible dictionary, Bible atlas, concordance, and one-volume Bible commentary together make for a good, basic reference library.

The Leader's Role

An effective leader prepares ahead. This leader guide provides easy to follow, step-by-step suggestions for leading a group. The key task of the leader is to guide discussion and activities that will engage heart and head and will invite faith development. Discussion questions are included, and you may want to add questions posed by you or your group. Here are suggestions for helping your group engage Scripture:

State questions clearly and simply.

Ask questions that move Bible truths from "outside" (dealing with concepts, ideas, or information about a passage) to "inside" (relating to the experiences, hopes, and dreams of the participants).

Work for variety in your questions, including compare and contrast, information recall, motivation, connections, speculation, and evaluation.

Avoid questions that call for yes-or-no responses or answers that are obvious.

Don't be afraid of silence during a discussion. It often yields especially thoughtful comments.

Test questions before using them by attempting to answer them yourself.

When leading a discussion, pay attention to the mood of your group by "listening" with your eyes as well as your ears.

Guidelines for the Group

IMMERSION is designed to promote full engagement with the Bible for the purpose of growing faith and building up Christian community. While much can be gained from individual reading, a group Bible study offers an ideal setting in which to achieve these aims. Encourage participants to bring their Bibles and read from Scripture during the session. Invite participants to consider the following guidelines as they participate in the group:

Respect differences of interpretation and understanding.

Support one another with Christian kindness, compassion, and courtesy.

Listen to others with the goal of understanding rather than agreeing or disagreeing.

Celebrate the opportunity to grow in faith through Bible study.

Approach the Bible as a dialogue partner, open to the possibility of being challenged or changed by God's Word.

Recognize that each person brings unique and valuable life experiences to the group and is an important part of the community.

Reflect theologically—that is, be attentive to three basic questions: What does this say about God? What does this say about me/us? What does this say about the relationship between God and me/us?

Commit to a *lived faith response* in light of insights you gain from the Bible. In other words, what changes in attitudes (how you believe) or actions (how you behave) are called for by God's Word?

Group Sessions

The group sessions, like the chapters themselves, are built around three sections: "Claim Your Story," "Enter the Bible Story," and "Live the Story." Sessions are designed to move participants from an awareness of their own life story, issues, needs, and experiences into an encounter and dialogue with the story of Scripture and to make decisions integrating their personal stories and the Bible's story.

The session plans in the following pages will provide questions and activities to help your group focus on the particular content of each chapter. In addition to questions and activities, the plans will include chapter title, Scripture, and faith focus.

Here are things to keep in mind for all the sessions:

Prepare Ahead
Study the Scripture, comparing different translations and perhaps a paraphrase.
Read the chapter, and consider what it says about your life and the Scripture.
Gather materials such as large sheets of paper or a markerboard with markers.
Prepare the learning area. Write the faith focus for all to see.

Welcome Participants
Invite participants to greet one another.
Tell them to find one or two people and talk about the faith focus.
Ask: What words stand out for you? Why?

Guide the Session
Look together at "Claim Your Story." Ask participants to give their reactions to the stories and examples given in each chapter. Use questions from the session plan to elicit comments based on personal experiences and insights.

Ask participants to open their Bibles and "Enter the Bible Story." For each portion of Scripture, use questions from the session plan to help participants gain insight into the text and relate it to issues in their own lives.

Step through the activity or questions posed in "Live the Story." Encourage participants to embrace what they have learned and to apply it in their daily lives.

Invite participants to offer their responses or insights about the boxed material in "Across the Testaments," "About the Scripture," and "About the Christian Faith."

Close the Session

Encourage participants to read the following week's Scripture and chapter before the next session.

Offer a closing prayer.

1. God's Ultimate Messenger
Hebrews 1–2

Faith Focus
What God has done in the past for us and continues even now through Jesus Christ is the foundation of our life of faith.

Before the Session
Before you begin your preparations for leading a study group in the Book of Hebrews, read the entire book at a single sitting. In many Bibles, this book is called the Letter to the Hebrews and is located with other letters in the New Testament. However, this book lacks many of the characteristics of first-century letters, leading some scholars to suggest that Hebrews is more like a sermon sent to a number of churches with the instruction that it be read aloud. Whatever its original form, this book emphasizes the significance of the new covenant in and through Jesus Christ.

Have a markerboard, or a large sheet of paper, and markers to use in the "Truly Human" section.

Claim Your Story

Most of us have heard about Jesus. You wouldn't be in this study group if you hadn't heard about Jesus! What have you heard, and what does it mean to you?

Form teams of three, and discuss: Who is Jesus, and what does he mean for me? How am I different because Jesus lived, died, was resurrected, and ascended to God?

Allow a few minutes for discussion, and then ask the teams to share a few of their answers.

Enter the Bible Story
Introduction
The study book writer states two reasons why the Book of Hebrews encourages people to listen to God's ultimate messenger, Jesus. Invite participants to identify those two reasons and to comment on whether these are still valid reasons to listen to Jesus Christ.

Ask: Are some Christians today "getting wobbly" about listening to—and obeying—Jesus? Give reasons and examples. Contrast reasons why the original readers of Hebrews were getting wobbly with reasons why contemporary Christians are getting wobbly.

The Majesty of Jesus

Review quickly the study book section on the majesty of Jesus. Then invite participants to identify in Hebrews 1:1-4 at least five characteristics or descriptions of Jesus that make that majesty clear.

Challenge participants to identify in verses 5-13 at least six ways in which Christ is superior to the angels.

Ask: What was the writer of Hebrews trying to assert in these verses? Did the writer make the case convincingly? Why did the writer of Hebrews make such a case for Jesus the Christ? (Hint: Look at Hebrews 2:1.) Is this still good counsel for us? Why?

A Reliable Message

In the study book, the "chain of authentication" is demonstrated from Jesus to the late first-century readers of Hebrews. Review "A Reliable Message" in the study book.

Ask: What is our chain of authentication? What validates our belief in the new covenant wrought through Christ? Is God still doing signs and wonders to verify the new covenant?

Invite participants to give reasons and illustrations. Ask: What convinced you to believe in Jesus Christ?

Truly Human

Jesus is superior to the angels, as Hebrews attests. However, in Hebrews 2:10-18, the writer of Hebrews made what for that time—and perhaps for our time—was an outlandish claim: Jesus is fully and truly human; and because he is truly human, we are saved by and through his suffering.

Ask: How can Jesus be wholly God and wholly human at the same time? (Hint: Don't expect a neat, precise answer. This is one of the ultimate paradoxes of the Christian faith. It is a fact that we accept on faith, not by logic or scientific proof.)

Jesus' humanity provides us with many benefits. As a group, review Hebrews 2:10-18. List on the markerboard or a large sheet of paper the specific benefits of Christ's humanity. Ask: Why did Jesus have to suffer? What for us is the effect of his suffering? Could he have accomplished his mission without suffering? Why?

Help participants perceive that Jesus chose to identify fully with human beings in order to save us from a life and an eternity of sinfulness. He had to identify fully with us so that we might have life abundant and life everlasting.

Ask participants to respond to this question from the study book: "In your own times of feeling as if you didn't belong, how has it helped you to know that Jesus calls you a member of his family?"

Live the Story

Hebrews is a rallying cry for passionate belief in and commitment to Jesus Christ. Ask your group to think about the important ways God speaks to us through Scriptures and through Jesus. Then invite participants to a time of silent prayer, each participant seeking a deeper commitment to and walk with Jesus the Christ. Confession may be in order for some in your group who may need to admit that their faith has been weak. Remind them that Christ knows and continues to love us.

2. Rest and Resistance
Hebrews 3–6

Faith Focus
Our faith is the key that makes us the recipients of God's promises, which are fulfilled in life today and in eternity.

Before the Session
Read Hebrews 3–6 and Chapter 2 in the study book. The writer of Hebrews used Old Testament Scriptures that were well-known to his or her audience, but may be less well-known to your group. Look up and read all the Old Testament passages cited in the text and in the study book so that they are fresh in your mind.

Locate a copy of the hymn "Trust and Obey," and share copies of the hymn with participants.

Are you praying for each member of your study group by name each day?

Claim Your Story

The study book focuses on the concept of rest in the chapter title and in the "Claim Your Story" section. The writer talks of rest as in need of sleep, time away, and relaxation. In teams of three, discuss the word *rest* and what it means for each person on the team.

Ask: What makes us feel unrested even when we've had enough sleep? In what ways can busy activity be draining? In what ways can it be restful and re-creating? In what ways can being surrounded by others be re-creating and restful? How would each team member define *rest*?

Enter the Bible Story

Enjoying God's Rest
Point out how the writer of Hebrews used familiar Old Testament stories to make her or his case. In Chapter 3, the writer used an incident from Israel's time in the wilderness as an example of resisting God and of missing out on God's perfect rest. Ask a participant to review the study book's account of this story quickly for the whole group.

Discuss: How did the Hebrews put God to the test during the Exodus? As significantly, why did they put God to the test? Ultimately, who was testing whom in the wilderness? What did God promise to those who passed the test?

A key word here is *rest*. What does *rest* mean to us? If rest is more than doing nothing, what other words come to mind for the concept of rest? Think about what the Hebrews were seeking during the Exodus. Does their story give new dimensions to the concept of rest? (Hint: If the group struggles with this, suggest that rest might involve a sense of peace, wholeness, quiet joy, and purposefulness. What other characteristics might participants add?)

Whenever We Are in Need

Ask: What, according to the writer of Hebrews, are the two great gifts God provided to help us enter his rest? (Hint: See Hebrews 4:12, 14.) If rest includes peace and joy, why do we not cling to it? More importantly, how can we lose that sense of peace and joy? Find an answer to this in Hebrews 4:11. Then the question becomes, What constitutes disobedience? How do we know if we are lapsing into disobedience? (Hint: The answer is in Hebrews 4:12-13,14.) Does this mean that each of us can read and interpret the Scriptures for ourselves? If not, who or what helps us in using the Scriptures as our guide?

Invite a participant to read Hebrews 4:15 aloud. As a whole group, discuss the meaning of this powerful verse. Ask: What does it mean for us that Christ was tested and tempted in every way that we have been tempted and tested? Part of an answer is contained in Hebrews 4:16.

A Call to Maturity

Invite participants to paraphrase or put into their own words Hebrews 5:11-14. Ask: What makes us "lazy" and in need (again?) of an introduction to the basics of God's message? How will we know when it is time to move on to the solid food of the gospel of Jesus Christ?

Read Hebrews 6:1 aloud. Ask: What is the meaning of spiritual maturity? How is it shown?

In teams of four, read Hebrews 6:4-8. Discuss the meaning of this passage. Use the study book for insights into the meaning of these verses. Why did the writer of Hebrews make such a categorical statement: "It's impossible"? Is it impossible, or was the writer making a point as emphatically as she or he could? Encourage participants to provide reasons for their answers.

Stern and frightening as these words are, the writer of Hebrews returned to the theme of hope and promise manifested in Christ Jesus. Work as a whole group to identify at least two (although there are more than two) indications in Hebrews 6:9-20 of the promises of God, promises of redemption and wholeness despite our sinfulness.

Invite participants to summarize in a single sentence the point of Hebrews 3–6.

Live the Story

Distribute copies of the hymn "Trust and Obey," and lead the group in singing it together. Then use the questions from the study book in "Live the Story" to help participants respond to the hymn.

Finally, invite participants to pray in silence as you read these sentences aloud, pausing for silent prayer between each sentence:

Lord, I have fallen away from you in these ways:

Lord, my heart has been unfaithful in these ways:

Lord, I need to encourage this person in the faith. Help me to know how to encourage with love and compassion.

Lord, I claim not only your rest but all of your promises, undeserving as I am.

Close with the Lord's Prayer.

3. A New Covenant
Hebrews 7:1–10:18

Faith Focus

God's gift of Jesus Christ to the world brings righteousness in place of sinfulness and joy in place of punishment.

Before the Session

This session will get into rather difficult material. First, there is the mysterious figure of Melchizedek, perhaps well-known to the original readers and hearers of Hebrews but less well-known to us. Second, there is an emphasis on the priesthood, so important in ancient Israel and in first-century Palestine but not much of a focus in our day.

While the Common English Bible is an excellent direct translation of Hebrews, the study book writer suggests that you can better understand this difficult section (Hebrews 7–10) by also reading it in a biblical paraphrase. Three good paraphrases include *The Message* (by Eugene H. Peterson), the *New Living Translation*, and the somewhat older *The New Testament in Modern English* (by J. B. Phillips). Your pastor may have one or more of these, and they are often available from public libraries.

Secure a markerboard, or a large piece of paper, and markers to use in the "Live the Story" section.

Claim Your Story

The writer for the study book speaks of how our understanding of and feelings about God have changed as we've matured and had various life experiences. She mentions that we may have come closer to God or pushed away from God or even done both. Invite participants to volunteer to talk about how their relationship to God has had ups and downs. Ask: What has made you feel closest to God?

Enter the Bible Story

A New Covenant

Form teams of three, and ask each team to consider these questions: What is a covenant? How is a covenant like a contract, and how is it different? What are some of the covenants of which we are a part? Are covenants always between two equal parties? Encourage participants to give reasons for their answers and provide examples or illustrations, if possible.

Here is how the first-century Jews likely heard the Christian claim of the covenant: For over 1,000 years, your people have believed—and you have been taught—that God has established a special covenant with your people, a permanent and everlasting covenant that cannot be broken or superseded. However, now people are teaching that God has established a new covenant, quite different from the first covenant, and that persons ought to commit themselves to this new covenant.

Ask: How would you feel if that message were directed to you? What might your response be? Could you surrender over 1,000 years of belief on the basis of what a few people claim is the new truth? Would you be willing to make that leap, to let go of what had been a sure thing for over 1,000 years to try something entirely new?

Allow time for participants to talk about their feelings as they ponder this.

A Different Kind of Priest

In teams of four, read Hebrews 7:1-28. Ask team members to list the differences between the ancient Hebrew high priests, including the mysterious Melchizedek, and Jesus Christ. Then invite them to share some of the ideas from the teams. As a whole group, discuss: Why did the writer of Hebrews want to compare and contrast Jesus with the high priests with which the first-century Jews were familiar? What point was the writer of Hebrews making here?

The study book writer summarizes this section by saying that the "new covenant is not based on law or regulations but on hope." Ask: What is this hope, and what does Jesus have to do with this hope?

Shadows and Substance

The hope in which the early Christians placed their trust was not just wishful thinking but a "startling new resonance." How had the new covenant, the new relationship with God, been manifested in their lives? How was—and is—Jesus the key to that covenant? How did this manifestation go far beyond the offering of sacrifices by the high priests?

Why All That Blood?

The study book writer points out that these chapters in Hebrews are filled with blood and sacrifices. Ask participants what the sacrifice of an animal might have meant to the early Hebrews. (Hint: Such an animal was the most valuable thing the individual had. What does this say about our offerings to God?) Blood was considered the center of life, much as we speak of the heart as being the center of life.

Ask: Why then does Hebrews refer to Christ as the new sacrifice? How might the shedding of Christ's blood on the cross help people raised on a sacrificial system understand the new covenant? Invite a participant to read Hebrews 10:10. How does this verse speak to the concept of sacrifice and the new covenant?

Live the Story

Ask a volunteer to read to the group the first two paragraphs of the "Live the Story" section from the study book. Discuss the questions in that section.

These chapters from Hebrews are filled with vital words and phrases: *Sacrifice, hope, new covenant, made holy.* Invite participants to add other key words and phrases. Write these on the markerboard or a large sheet of paper. Then ask each participant to offer her or his own silent prayer, using some of these words.

4. Promise and Pain
Hebrews 10:19-39

Faith Focus

Once redeemed, we are able to walk on Jesus' path to the glorious completion of God's promise.

Before the Session

While the passage to be considered is comparatively brief, it is important. Try this to help your understanding of the passage: Summarize in a sentence or two Hebrews 10:19-25, verses 26-31, and verses 31-39. Use this outline as you lead your study group in this session.

Claim Your Story

Invite a volunteer to read aloud the first paragraph of the "Claim Your Story" section of the study book, and then ask participants to reflect silently as you read the following questions aloud. Pause to let participants think after each question. Do not ask for reports from any participants, but explain that these questions represent the gist of the passage from Hebrews under consideration.

What does it mean, in times of discouragement, to have faith?

How do you access Jesus' "new and living way"? What help can you expect to find?

When did you first claim the salvation Jesus Christ offers to all?

What kinds of situations in your life have caused you to stray from the covenant with God through Christ? What has taken place that has led you into sinful actions, words, and thoughts?

Who or what has encouraged you to "get right with God" again after you strayed? How have you helped others return to the covenant of grace through Jesus Christ?

In what ways does God's will make room for adverse events?

The *CliffNotes* Hebrews

The study book writer suggests that these 21 verses represent a summary of the entire Book of Hebrews. Ask: According to the study book, what was happening in the lives of the persons to whom Hebrews was written that they needed this summary? How is what was transpiring in their lives similar to what takes place in our lives from time to time?

Invite participants to recall a time when "it seemed your faith was doing you no good at all." If participants would like to share thoughts on this, allow them to do so; but do not press anyone for a response.

Act on Your Confidence

The passage of Scripture claims that we have confidence in the blood of Jesus. Ask: What makes us confident? How do we act if we are confident? What kinds of actions suggest that we are not confident?

According to the study book writer, the proof of our confidence is in the doing, not just in the saying. Ask participants to list at least five things that those who are confident will do as a result. The study book writer lists these; but ask participants to identify them from the biblical text, using the study book section only if these five cannot be located. (They include drawing near to God [10:22], holding on to our faith [10:23], motivating one another to show love [10:24], continuing to mee together [10:25a], and encouraging one another [10:25b].) Ask: How do you practice these five today?

The Fear Factor

Ask: Can Christians become so confident in God's love that they feel they are free to do as they please? Invite a good reader to read aloud Hebrews 10:26-31. Ask: What is the point of this passage? What is the writer of Hebrews trying to tell his or her readers—and us?

The study book writer points out that the writer of Hebrews was not talking about making mistakes or doing things we ought not to do or leaving undone things we should do. What kinds of mistakes was the writer of Hebrews describing? Ask participants to identify three kinds of sin that the writer of Hebrews described as "a decision to sin" (10:26). Then invite them to define and give examples of each of these three. (Hint: The three kinds of sin can be found in verse 29.)

Encourage participants to give specific examples of each of these kinds of sin: How do we walk all over God's Son? How do we act as if the blood of Christ is "ordinary" blood? How do we insult the Spirit of grace?

Live Up to Your Own Example

The third section of these 21 verses is strong on encouragement. What did the writer of Hebrews suggest the readers do for encouragement? (Hint: Live up to their own previous example.) Does that same source of encouragement affect us as well? On what can we depend if we become discouraged by what is happening to us? How can we learn to trust that new covenant, the "blood of Christ," in the midst of trials and failures?

Live the Story

Ask a participant to read aloud the first two paragraphs of the "Live the Story" section from the study book. Invite the group as a whole to discuss the question at the end of the second paragraph.

Next, form teams of three. Then invite participants to describe for other team members a time when they were tempted by life to fall away from faith in Christ and to identify what and/or who helped bring them back to confidence in Christ.

Close by asking the whole group to pray the Lord's Prayer.

5. Seeing the Unseen
Hebrews 11

Faith Focus

Models of faithfulness help us live worthy lives and give us hope to reach the final goal.

Before the Session

Hebrews 11 catalogs some of the heroes of the faith from Israel's history. Prophets, kings, and commoners are mentioned here as examples of those who kept the faith against great odds. Look up those heroes who may be less than familiar to you, and get a sense of how faith operated in their lives. (See the study book for the biblical references.) Then, as you lead the group during this session, feel free to summarize the stories of faith of some of these lesser-known champions of the faith highlighted in this chapter.

Claim Your Story

Start by discussing the questions the study book raises in the "Claim Your Story" section: What are some of the things you have been told, or have thought, about faith? Have you wondered or worried at all about your own faith? What does Hebrews 11:1 mean for the way we lives our lives? Does "the reality of what we hope for" mean that we will get everything for which we hope? If not, what does it mean?

Enter the Bible Story

Look at What Faith Can Do

The writer of Hebrews called upon the history of the Hebrew people to demonstrate the power and place of faith.

As a whole group, call out the names of those listed in Chapter 11 as heroes of faith. If any of these biblical heroes are unknown to some participants, take a moment to tell their stories.

Ask: For which of these heroes was clinging to the faith difficult? Which of these heroes faced great adversity for their faith? What do the stories of these heroes tell us today about clinging to faith in the face of adversity? The study book writer describes the adversities persons of faith face in our time. How are these adversities different from those faced by the heroes listed in Chapter 11? Is the subtle, seductive adversity we face more or less challenging than the life and death adversities faced by the heroes of faith? Encourage participants to give reasons for their answers.

Invite participants to a moment of silent reflection in response to this question: How are you making your faith visible to the persons who surround you every day?

A Way of Seeing

The study book writer points out that faith is "a way of seeing the world, of framing our experience." However, the faith way of seeing, of framing, is God-centered, not human-centered. As a whole group, discuss: What makes you think that different people see the world and frame experience differently from those individuals listed in Hebrews 11? What are some of the ways that are not God-centered? What are some of the ways popular culture tells us to see the world and frame our experience?

What does "by faith we understand that the universe has been created by a word from God" mean in terms of seeing the world and framing experience?

Real People, Real World

We might assume that only perfect, holy persons can live by the kind of faith that Hebrews describes; but invite participants to look again at the list of biblical heroes cited in this chapter. Ask: How many of these were "perfect" persons? How many of these never made a mistake? How many of these lived lives free from temptation and sin? What do the group's responses to these questions say to us today—and to our potential for being heroes of faith for others?

Taking the Long View

The study book writer states unequivocally that God wins in the end and that those who trust in God will triumph. Ask: Since the heroes of faith in Chapter 11 couldn't see the end, what did they see that kept them going in faith? If we cannot see the end, what is it that we do see and experience that keeps us trusting in God and living in faith?

Summarize: This is what faith is: seeing only a small part of the picture but believing totally in the Creator of the picture and trusting that the day will come when we see the whole—and thus, we live by faith.

Live the Story

Form teams of four. Ask participants to tell their team members about their personal heroes of faith (relatives, friends, and mentors) whose faith has encouraged them to live lives of faith.

After team members have had an opportunity to talk about their faith heroes, reassemble as a whole group and discuss these questions: What did all of these faith heroes have in common? In what ways did these faith heroes make their faith visible and obvious?

Invite participants to offer silent prayers, opening themselves fully to God's presence and committing themselves to live by faith.

6. Staying the Course With Jesus
Hebrews 12–13

Faith Focus

Bringing the grace of God to all in the community and persevering toward the goal of eternity puts us in company with Jesus.

Before the Session

Summarize in one to three sentences the major learnings you have gleaned from Hebrews. You will be asking participants to do the same later, but do not judge their summaries by your own. Scripture speaks to each of us in different ways because each of us brings to the Word our own life situations.

Arrange to have a markerboard, or a large sheet of paper, and markers to use in the "Hard Training" section.

Claim Your Story

Ask a volunteer to read aloud the "Claim Your Story" section from the study book. Invite participants to give examples of where they learned foundational skills that they have later employed in useful ways. Then explain that the closing pages of Hebrews sketch out for us basic attitudes and practices on which to ground a well-lived Christian life.

Enter the Bible Story

To Run Freely in Faith

The study book writer points out that sin is a weight that clings to us, preventing us from running the race, living the life that we ought to experience. Form teams of three, and then ask the following questions from the study book: What "extra baggage is compromising your discipleship at this moment? What would it take to strip that away?" If some on the teams of three are uncomfortable, do not push them to respond. Some may be more comfortable talking about a sin that they laid aside in the past rather than focusing on the present. Hear from those teams that are willing to respond.

Hard Training

As a whole group, discuss ways in which hardships and difficulties have strengthened participants. Then work on the concept of discipline. Ask: What is discipline? How is discipline different from punishment? How does God discipline us? Can we distinguish between the discipline that God places upon us and the discipline we might receive from natural events? How? Encourage participants to give reasons for their answers. (Hint: Help participants recognize that God's discipline is often internal—the sense of guilt we feel when we have failed God—while naturally occurring discipline is more often external. Then affirm that we are equipped by grace to handle and grow from any discipline.)

The study book writer states that the Book of Hebrews provides a number of tips to prevent "career-ending faith injuries." Ask participants to call these out while you write them on the markerboard or a large sheet of paper. Note how many of these are dependent on the Christian community. Highlight these, then ask: Is our Christian community doing a good job of helping one another in these ways? Encourage participants to give reasons for their answers.

Making the Choice

The writer of Hebrews sets out alternatives in stark terms. We are either part of the new covenant or we are not. Ask: Whose choice is it to be part of the covenant? What is the result of refusing to make a choice at all? Help participants see that Hebrews is demanding a conscious choice on the part of each person.

Significantly, the writer of Hebrews argues that the choice we make is reflected not in what we say but in what we do. Ask: Do we do the things that the writer of Hebrews discusses—hospitality to strangers, moral behavior, not idolizing money—to gain favor with God? If we do not do these things to gain God's favor, then why do we do them? Encourage participants to give reasons for their answers.

Help participants recognize that Christ wants us to live the Christian life not in fear of what God will do if we don't, but in grateful response to what God has already done for us in Christ. Ask: How does this speak to the choice to be part of the covenant?

Outside the Camp

The Book of Hebrews concludes with a warning to beware of strange teachings. Invite teams of four to read Hebrews 13:7-16, and then discuss how we can determine if a new idea is a "strange teaching." Many strange teachings are circulating, even within Christian churches. Ask: How can we be sure we are not being seduced by these? What is the basic truth to which we must cling?

Allow time for the teams to respond.

Live the Story

As part of your preparation for this session, you jotted down the major learnings you gleaned from Hebrews in one to three sentences. Now ask participants to do the same. When all have written down their sentences, gather in teams of four and share these sentences. Remember, not all have to agree. The Scriptures speak to each of us personally.

Close with a prayer of thanksgiving for the Book of Hebrews, for the Scriptures themselves, and for each member of the study group.

BIBLIOGRAPHY

Bibles

Aland, Kurt, Matthew Black, Carlo M. Martini, Bruce M. Metzger, and Allen Wikgren, ed. *The Greek New Testament*. Third edition (corrected). Stuttgart: United Bible Societies, 1966.

Brenton, Sir Lancelot C.L. *The Septuagint With Apocrypha: Greek and English*. 1851; rpt. Peabody, MA: Hendrickson Publishers, 1986.

Holy Bible. New International Version. New York International Bible Society, 1973.

Holy Bible. New Living Translation. Wheaton, IL: Tyndale Charitable Trust, 1996.

New Testament. Common English Bible. Common English Bible, 2010.

Nouveau Testament. Traduction Œcuménique de la Bible. Édition intégrale. Société biblique française—Les Éditions du Cerf, 1972.

Peterson, Eugene H. *The Message: The Bible in Contemporary Language*. Colorado Springs, CO: NavPress, 2004.

Snaith, Norman Henry, ed. *Sēfer Tōrah N^{e}vi'im Uk^{e}thuvim* (Hebrew Old Testament). London: The British and Foreign Bible Society, 1977.

The Bible. Contemporary English Version. American Bible Society, 1995.

The Holy Bible. New Revised Standard Version. Division of Christian Education of the National Council of the Churches of Christ in the United States of America, 1989.

Commentaries and Reference

Achtemeier, Elizabeth. *Nahum–Malachi*. Ed. James Luther Mays. Interpretation: A Bible Commentary for Teaching and Preaching. Atlanta, GA: John Knox Press, 1986.

Allen, Leslie C. *Psalms 101–150*. Ed. David A. Hubbard, Glenn W. Barker. Word Biblical Commentary, Vol. 21. Waco, TX: Word, 1983.

Coleman, Lyman, Denny Rydberg, Richard Peace, Gary Christopherson, ed. *The Serendipity Bible Study Book*. Grand Rapids, MI: Zondervan Publishing House, 1986.

D'Angelo, Mary Rose. "Hebrews." *Women's Bible Commentary: expanded edition with Apocrypha*. Ed. Carol A. Newsom and Sharon H. Ringe. Louisville, KY: Westminster John Knox Press,1992, 1998.

Dosick, Rabbi Wayne. *Living Judaism: The Complete Guide to Jewish Belief, Tradition, and Practice*. New York: HarperCollins, 1995.

Fuller, Reginald H. "The Letter to the Hebrews." *Hebrews, James, 1 and 2 Peter, Jude, Revelation* Ed. Gerhard Krodel. Proclamation Commentaries: The New Testament Witnesses for Preaching. Philadelphia, PA: Fortress Press, 1977.

Guthrie, Donald. *Hebrews*. Ed. Leon Morris. The Tyndale New Testament Commentaries. Grand Rapids, MI: William B. Eerdmans Publishing Company, 1983.

Guthrie, George H. "Hebrews." *Zondervan Illustrated Bible Backgrounds Commentary, volume 4: Hebrews to Revelation*. Ed. Clinton E. Arnold. Grand Rapids, MI: Zondervan, 2002.

Haber, Susan. "From Priestly Torah to Christ Cultus: The Re-Vision of Covenant and Cult in Hebrews." *Journal for the Study of the New Testament* 28.1 (2005), pp. 105-124.

Hahn, Scott. "Covenant in the Old and New Testaments: Some Current Research (1994-2004)." *Currents in Biblical Research* 3.2 (2005), pp. 263-292.

Harrison, R.K. *Leviticus*. Ed. D.J. Wiseman. The Tyndale Old Testament Commentaries. Downers Grove, IL: Inter-Varsity Press, 1980.

Joslin, Barry C. "Can Hebrews be Structured? An Assessment of Eight Approaches." *Currents in Biblical Research* 6.1 (2007), pp. 99-129.

Livingstone, Elizabeth A., ed. *The Concise Oxford Dictionary of the Christian Church*. Oxford: Oxford University Press, 1977.

Okure, Teresa. "Hebrews: Sacrifice in an African Perspective." *Global Bible Commentary*. Ed. Daniel Patte. Nashville, TN: Abingdon Press, 2004.

Perry, Peter S. "Making Fear Personal: Hebrews 5:11 - 6:12 and the Argument from Shame." *Journal for the Study of the New Testament* 32.1 (2009), pp. 100-125.

Purdy, Alexander C. and J. Harry Cotton. "Hebrews." Ed. George Arthur Buttrick. *The Interpreter's Bible, volume XI: Philippians, Colossians, Thessalonians,*

Timothy, Titus, Philemon, Hebrews. Nashville, TN: Abingdon Press, 1955.
Richards, Lawrence O. The Teacher's Commentary. Wheaton, IL: Victor Books (a division of Scripture Press), 1987.

Schiffman, Lawrence H. Understanding Second Temple and Rabbinic Judaism. Ed. Jon Bloomberg and Samuel Kapustin. Jersey City, NJ: Ktav Publishing House, Inc., 2003.

Tofan, Stelian. "Hebrews." Global Bible Commentary. Ed. Daniel Patte. Nashville, TN: Abingdon Press, 2004.

Zerwick, Max, and Mary Grosvenor. A Grammatical Analysis of the Greek New Testament. Revised edition. Rome: Biblical Institute Press, 1981.